MY
LANDY-LIFE

Enjoy reading my tales.

Martin D Smith

MY
LANDY-LIFE
with Landy-Luck

Martin Smithson

GSP

My Landy-Life
Martin Smithson

Published by Greyhound Self-Publishing 2019
Malvern, Worcestershire, United Kingdom.

Printed and bound by Aspect Design
89 Newtown Road, Malvern, Worcs. WR14 1PD
United Kingdom
Tel: 01684 561567
E-mail: allan@aspect-design.net
Website: www.aspect-design.net

Cover Design Copyright © 2019 Martin Smithson
Original photograph Martin Smithson © 2019
ISBN 978-1-909219-61-8

Contents

Chapter 1

My Conversion to a Landy Life

Land Rover claim to be the 'Best 4x4 by Far'. Just live with one for a while and soon you will realize just how true that is. Each one, just like we simple humans, has a certain charm, and its own special quirks. Each has its very own individual foibles and imperfections; along with personal characters, fascinations and appeals. Occasionally, they may be stubborn and somewhat temperamental. Living with a Landy is akin to a marriage. Long-term relationships require bonding, blended with a dose of 'give and take' to succeed. Be wary though as Landys can and frequently do, take over your life. You become secretly driven into their wonderful world of Landy-Life. Once tempted you never look back. It could even be at the price of other unions in your life.

A Land Rover, without question is the best vehicle on, or off, the road. However, like so many of we humans they are prone, from time to time, to become obstinate and noncompliant; at least in the eye of the operator behind the wheel.

Most incidences of obstinacy or non-compliance can, to greater or lesser extent, be put down to 'operator error'. How often do you hear of a Land Rover said to have 'broken down'? Such indictments are quite untrue. They go more places and suffer more hard use and abuse than anything else on four wheels would ever be expected to tolerate. It's not surprising then that 'Progress may, now and then, become Temporarily Impeded' or **PTI,** as I call these hiccups. Don't worry, as Landy friends and the watchful Landy-Luck, usually come along to help should your progress ever become Temporarily Impeded. I have lived the Landy-Life and loved Land Rovers with all their Landy ways for many years.

Allow me to explain about my transition to the 'Landy-Life' and a few of the many on-going 'experiences' of Land Rovers on and off-roading and overlanding. I will share with you some of those special times when the unexpected happens.

Very occasionally Landy relationships do break down, usually with later regret. Just as we drive the bumpy road of life and perhaps straying 'off-road' now and again. I have lived with a few of these 'off-road temptresses', despite the many warnings and threats from other close quarters. Fear not though, a Landy will soon find you many more friends.

My first Landy relationship was as a lad in an old 1960s Series 1 on a friend's farm. The cattle and sheep living out in the fields never got so much food and attention. The seed was then sown to gradually grow, blossom and germinate in the fullness of time.

Some year's later, Christine and I with our three children were living in a remote farmhouse, a mile off the road in Lancashire. My off-roading chariot at the time was a Daihatsu 4x4.

One snowy winters morning I went out to start her up; there was no sign of the Daihatsu, it was completely buried under a snow drift. I dug it out, got it going and drove off through the deep snow. Not getting far, the engine cut out; despite my many attempts it would not re-start. Investigating, I found the fuel supply had been cut off by the plastic fuel pipe that had been squashed by frozen snow. Getting very cold hands I managed to sort it.

Later Christine walked the mile down the lane through the snow to buy milk from the village shop. I was flabbergasted when she returned with a gem of a 1972, ex-police, three door Range Rover. She had met a local Landy man in the shop who just happened to have the RR at his farm, where he worked on

Land Rovers. That must have been the most expensive pint of milk ever!

Not realising at the time, it was as if a multi-purpose fertilizer had been spread over the now germinating Landy seed sown all those years earlier. Harvest time for me came in the early 80s, during the time of the famous Camel Trophy [1981 to 2000]; an annual challenge event sponsored by Land Rover and Camel Cigarettes. Competitors from around the world took part in what became known as the 'Olympics' of the 4x4 world.

The competition involved teams doing extreme Land Rovering in remote locations. Over the years it took them to Argentina, Zaire, Brazil, Borneo, Chile, Sumatra, Indonesia, Siberia, Australia, USSR and Burundi to name just a few of the many locations.

Selection and training was carried out in the grounds of the Eastnor Castle Estate near Ledbury. Land Rover runs testing and Land Rover Experience Day promotions and various other shows at Eastnor Castle Estate to this day. Training and final selection took place during the cold winter months of January and February of each year. Contenders were obliged to sleep onsite under canvass during those cold wet weeks of their induction.

The instructors were more fortunate as they stayed in the warmth and comfort of the nearby Guest House which Christine and I owned at the time. When many wonderfully enjoyable short nights and early mornings were relished, along with much camaraderie and washing of clothes and gear. For sure, this was the time I became fully converted to the way of Landy-Life

At those times when things do go wrong, or perhaps don't go as planned, as they may from time to time, the Landy usually carries the blame. Of course, Landys take it all in their stride without so much as a complaint, grumble or murmur. After all the poor Landy can't answer back. This befits we 'operators' very well as it makes us feel, quite mistakenly, more powerful in a controlling and somehow superior kind of way. Most such incidences experienced of Land Rover non-cooperation, non-compliance, or any other such mulishness as we might call it are in fact brought about through 'operator' error. Often you hear of a Land Rover having 'broken down' or 'gotten stuck'.

Every Landy Lover knows only too well that they rarely break down or get stuck as such. True Landy converts are positive and would never consider using the words 'broken down' or 'stuck'. It is just an instance of **P**rogress becoming **T**emporarily **I**mpeded or (**PTI**).

This terminology goes a long way toward upholding Land Rover's reputation and the operator's Landy-Life ego; it also nurtures the relationship between machine and driver. No Land Rover could ever get itself in any difficult situation without an 'operator'. Co-operation between the Land Rover and driver is crucial for recovery from any **PTI** with one's dignity and self-esteem intact. Each one is a unique 'operator' experience helping toward getting to know your Landy more intimately. Whenever and wherever you encounter a Land Rover **PTI,** those Landy friends are sure to come to your aide, if only to enjoy the experience with you. It is uncanny how those Landy friends turn up when you need them; Landy-Luck also plays a part.

Just occasionally though, especially when you have been particularly brainless, you may well wish they would evaporate. We've all been there!

One time, when in a desolate part of western Namibia in my very thirsty and heavily 'tweaked' V8 Discovery1, I experienced an **O**ut of **F**uel **PTI (OFPTI).** Expecting a long wait under the blisteringly hot sun my mate and I sheltered in the shade of the only tree to be found. No more than five minutes passed by when Landy-Luck brought along a passing Land Rover that willingly towed us the 50km or so to the nearest filling station. The timing was perfect, and we were indeed very lucky as we filled our tanks and jerry cans with the very last drop of fuel left in their pumps. Many litres of Landy-Luck descended upon us that day. Just one customer ahead of us would have landed us with a problem as it was Friday afternoon; no fuel deliveries were due until next Monday.

There is a much-voiced saying that "80% of the Land Rovers ever built are still on the road while the other 20% got home". This is an immense untruth, as all Land Rover owners know only too well! Every Landy is perfectly capable of 'getting home'. Some may need a degree of encouragement and TLC; and perhaps also a measure of Landy-Luck to reach home. Sometimes it may take months or perhaps years of grafting and overhauling, accompanied by varying degrees of physical and mental stress. Not to mention the more than anticipated 'pocket mining'. Once home a Landy becomes a truly happy, friendly, useful and worthwhile member of the family. I feel sorry for those that don't have the pleasure of such a treasure. Sadly, they just don't know what they are missing.

PTIs come in various guises, the list is endless. Each is a lesson helping to make life more interesting, exciting, rewarding and memorable. I'll share with you some of the many '**PTI**s' I've enjoyed over years in different locations.

For each worthy **PTI** I award my version of the **C**amel **T**rophy **M**edal (**CTM**). The award I conceived to help recall memories of the Camel Trophy for those people, places, pleasures and sacrifices met and enjoyed along the happy road of Landy-Life.

Chapter 2
My Landy Family

At the time of writing the family members included:-

Airportable Lightweight, Series111 - Boudie.

Named after the charioting 'off-roader' who in Roman times dealt many a blow to the then invading Romans.

Boudie

Discovery1 300 tdi, Tasca.

A daughter of Boudicca's. A long serving and faithful family member. Still going strong having been de-winched and de-cluttered she is now enjoying her semi-retirement.

Tasca

Defender 110 300 tdi Kalahari.

A limited-edition model made at the time of the launch of the TD5 Defender. Basically, it is a TD5 fitted with the about to be ceased 300tdi engine and running gear.

Kalahari

The Kalahari was produced between 2002 and 2005 to satisfy demand from South Africa for an over-lander without all the electronic gizmos the newer generations seem to insist on imposing upon owners. The Kalahari remained a 'proper' Land Rover. It could be 'fixed' in the bush; a big plus for hammer and screwdriver mechanics like me, or at least as I claim to be! Though I rather suspect at the time there were several about to be made redundant 300tdi engines and running gear left lying around the Lode Lane factory with no home to go to. For what it's worth, I rate the 300tdi as the best engine Land Rover ever made. Sadly, the distinctive Kalahari side decals were removed before mine joined my Landy family and I've not yet managed to find replacements.

Other family members include a **2009-Freelander2** which, along with a **2007-Defender 110-Puma,** live in England along with Tasca the Disco1; that is when she's at home!

A while back I had to split the family up as they constantly argued over who should take me for a drive. So Boudle the Lightweight was taken to my home in South Africa where she lived happily alongside my Defender Kalahari already domiciled there. How she got there is another tale to be told.

Thankfully they got on very well together, entertaining me when and wherever we went; more about that later.

I confess to having had several dirty Landy affairs over the years. Most of those relationships broke down for diverse reasons. Just like real life! Past liaisons included a V8 Discovery1 – a Discovery3 – and a Range Rover along with several other hybrid 'off-roaders'. They were all great fun at the time.

Long may the family live happily together, in which or whatever direction they may take!

Thank you, Land Rover for the great variety of wonderful **Land Rover 'experiences'.**

Chapter 3
How Boudie joined the family

I was at home in Castlemorton, Worcestershire messing about in Land Rovers as usual, when Landy-Luck whispered into my ear sweet words about an abandoned ex RAF SeriesIII Airportable Lightweight. It was once FFR (fitted for radio) and living in the hedge of the garden next door to a family friend. Calling the friend, I learnt the owner would like to part with this beauty and that he needed a garden shed

I coveted that Lwt which had been rusting away in the hedge for the past six years or more. It so happened that my friend, the owner's neighbour, was looking to be rid of a garden shed that was sitting on the boundary between the two homes. Without wasting a moment, with my friend 'Fixer', we winched the shed from one garden to the next, loaded the Lwt onto a trailer and away we went. Didn't I say that when in need of Landy help a friend and Landy-Luck always turn up?

Minutes later we off-loaded my new-found treasure at my home. Fuelled her up; the batteries were flat of course, so we gave it a tow; not for one moment expecting it to spark into life. Well believe it or not, after about five meters of towing, once the brakes had freed up and with the help of Landy-Luck, she was healthily firing on all four. Off we went for a short spin around the block. I came back grinning from ear to ear, checked her over, just not believing how, after such a long period of neglect, she was performing so well. Just another one of the 80% of those Landys ever made that reached home with just a little time, TLC and a pinch of help from Landy-

Luck! With less than 20,000 miles recorded on the clock she was now a welcome member of the family.

Ideas kept pouring into my head of things 'out of the ordinary' to do with this amazing Landy. An overland adventure might perhaps be a good idea? I kept dreaming of plans for some sort of trip. Work was carried out to help her cope with what may lie ahead and for the off-road life I was about to introduce her to.

ARB diff lockers were fitted front and rear. A snorkel was added, a winch mounted up front and sand ladders fixed to the sides of the rear tub. Twin batteries were installed to ensure an ample power for the now added winch and possibly a fridge in the future. I also fitted an inverter, making Boudie AC/DC. She was given a new coat in the form of a canvass tilt, which at the second attempt fitted perfectly.

With that done, I took her a few times to the then popular 'Tommy's, great off-road site in the Welsh hills near Rhayader also to the Strata Florida trail, amongst others. They were great times; Boudie behaved impeccably!

Still ideas were flooding through my head. I found she would go almost anywhere, through mud, crevices, rivers, up and down waterfalls. You name it wherever I aimed her she would willingly go; what's more she always came back. I managed to break a rear half shaft a few times; each soon fixed, I carried spares cable-tied to the chassis to fix these, self-inflicted '**S**hafting' **PTI. (SPTI)**

So far so good - what more could I do for her. The original heavy-duty cart springs were changed for a set of softer parabolic springs. What a difference that made, she became a much more comfortable chariot. An internal Roll bar was made up and fitted. A rear spare wheel carrier, with bracketry for a Highlift jack, shovel and pick axe, were attached. To facilitate this the tail gate was altered to become a hinged door.

Also, a bonnet top spare wheel carrier was added to carry the all-important extra spare wheel. A second-hand Fairey overdrive I bought and fitted made substantial differences especially to third and fourth gears by reducing both revs and fuel consumption. A higher third gear proved most useful, especially when climbing long gradients.

Sadly, the paintwork had suffered over those years she spent living in the hedge. Landy-Luck obviously had been looking after her as the bulkhead, unusually, was relatively rot-free. With the minor rust dealt with the bodywork was re-sprayed in Land Rover Camel Trophy Sand Glow Yellow. She did look good in her new colour. It was now that I christened her 'Boudicca' or 'Boudie' for short.

The idea of some sort of adventure was still turning over and over even more persistently in my mind. I have a home in South Africa, so decided to set a goal of making an overland trip from UK to South Africa in her.

That leads on to more **PTI** tales.

Chapter 4
Kalahari Steering

Darkness approaches, the lions are hungry, their dinner time is looming! Here we are, 'Fixer and me, in the Kalahari Desert, driving my 1996 V8 Discovery1. We are on our way back from Maun, in Botswana, to our tent we left, three days earlier, at an 'informal' campsite in the Desert. The reason for the visit to Maun was to replace a faulty power-steering pump. After

I'm Hungry

eventually getting a new pump fitted, we lost all steering on our way back. We called on Landy-Luck to help us cope.

The tracks here are merely ruts in the sand. Straight line driving, with no steering was not a problem as the ruts did the work. However, the route back to our tent, which we had left three days earlier, challenged us with many twists and turnoffs along the 150km or so left to go. One of us would be on the outside coaxing the front wheels into taking the correct track ahead and not follow the easier straight-ahead route. We took it in turns to be on the outside 'enticing' and 'persuading' the Landy to take the right direction. The luckier one was driving and keeping a wary eye out for hungry prowling lions. Those ruts that normally make desert driving a delight now reaped a hefty refund from us.

Picture the scene; herds of grazing Gemsbok, Springbok, Zebras, Hartebeest and other 'lion dinners' in the Lions pantry, ready for eating. To be certain not to be on the lion's menu we scanned around to ensure not to be listed as 'the

A lion slaughtered Cheetah

succulent human starter' for that evening's lion family banquet. Something had recently made our awareness even more acute. Leaving camp, those few days before, we came across a Cheetah carcass that had been taken down and torn apart by a lion and left for the vultures to feast upon. Apparently, this is normal practice for Lions to help reduce the competition from other predators that enjoy the same spread that they savour. It was the scores of vultures flapping and squawking that attracted our attention to the carcass. We weren't concerned about vultures as I was told they only eat dead meat; something we hoped not to become.

Once back at Camp the cause of the now **'No Steering' PTI (NSPTI)** we found to be a broken steering column. The splines at the upper end of the steering column had stripped inside the steel clamp of the universal joint. 'Fixer' had the brilliant idea of reversing the UJ, filing down the sides of the clamp to give more grip and leverage when re-tightened. Amazingly the 'fix' worked well, given our limited tool resource with of course, a little help from Landy-Luck. We then continued to enjoy our jaunt through the Kalahari and onward through South Africa all the way back to Cape Town, some 2,000km, or more without a further glitch.

It's so easy to blame Land Rover, especially as we were later told the aluminium steering columns were used only for a few years, around 1996. Had we known, would we have done anything about it beforehand? It wouldn't have entered our heads!

Soon after we set out on the trip the power-steering began causing us grief, working only intermittently, making driving difficult. Eventually the pump gave up the ghost altogether, hence the visit to Land Rover Maun to fix this **'S**teering **P**ump' **PTI. (SPPTI).** Yes, we did regularly check the steering fluid levels, keeping the level to the lower mark allowing for the fluid to expand as it warmed up!

The trek to Maun was not easy with our overloaded Disco. She was packed to the gunnels with a roof-rack, sand-ladders and supplementary fuel tank. Not to mention four full jerry cans of fuel and the 40 litre of water in an under-floor tank. This plus a full 40 litre fridge, a cool box, and high-lift jack, along with a plethora of other necessary and even more unnecessary gear and 'junk' one carts overland. This is what happens when you listen to all the advice, the good and the not so good, and read in journals and advertisements as to what 'must' be taken on-board. Advice given with the best of intentions I am sure.

I now have my own list of 'bare necessities'.

We left camp to visit the Land Rover Garage in the town of Maun, some 200km away to the north, leaving behind our ten travelling companions and their Landys. We were acting upon the recommendation of our well known Landy friend and guru, Schalk Burger, who with his wife Marlize runs a great independent Landy business in Somerset West. They have been keeping my SA Landys rolling for some sixteen or more years. We set off early in the morning expecting to make it a one-day round trip to quickly change the power steering pump.

The journey to Maun was pleasant enough, we made the best we could of the sandy drive with the intermittent power-steering. At the Maun Land Rover garage, we were greeted by very helpful and pleasant staff, even though, unbeknown to us, it was a local bank holiday! Despite this, the helpfulness of everyone was remarkable. They took us on a tour around the town. I bought a great tool roll from The Kalahari Canvass Company where we spent time looking around their factory where they fabricate a wide range of canvass and leather items.

Should you need a new canvass hood or a tent; they are fantastic. The tool roll has been with me in my successive Land Rovers ever since, in fact I never drive my Landy in Africa without it under my seat. They kindly checked us into a local Hotel, where we dined on Crocodile and enjoyed the town's nightlife. It was a most pleasant night spent in luxury, in fact a luxurious **B**ank **H**oliday **PTI (BHPTI)**; not that our tents and sleeping bags back at camp are anything

Next day the power-steering pump was proclaimed to be 'beyond repair'. No problem they declared, as a new one will be flown overnight from the main Land Rover dealer, over 500kms away, in Gaborone. We had no issue with that, as we spent a pleasant rest of the day and another enjoyable night in Maun.

Next morning, we waited at the local airstrip for the plane to arrive at the scheduled 10:30am. Well, true to African time keeping, 10:30 came and went, so we waited and waited! Eventually, an hour or so later, we were told the plane had not yet left Gaborone; apparently the pilot hadn't shown up for work as he had overslept! It would now arrive at 'about' 4pm; not unusual for Africa. A simple case of a '**P**lane **D**elay' **(PDPTI)**.

This reminded me of the adage that goes:-

"The Swiss may have invented the clock,
but don't forget that the Africans own the time".

At the Land Rover garage, I spotted a row of eight dusty, nearly new Discos, bearing strange number plates lined up against the back wall of the yard as if on parade. I suggested we might 'loan' a power-steering pump from one of those vehicles, which could be replaced with the new pump when it arrived from Gaborone. The immediate reaction was a very definite "No".

I then discovered those Discos had been parked up there for more than a year, having come on exercise as part of a UN exercise from across the South African border.

The engine of each Disco was damaged by, according to Land Rover, 'Bad Fuel'. They were being held there for the duration of a long on-going dispute, between the SA army and Land Rover over the fuel used. Apparently, the UN brought their own fuel supply with them into the country in a bowser to keep them fuelled up; hence the dispute. It goes without saying that eventually we ended up with a power-steering pump from one of those sad vehicles; it proved faultless.

The cause of the later broken steering column', on our way back to camp, was partly due to our new-found confidence in the now amazing steering. The energy deployed, combined with the misuse and overloading we had inflicted upon it by driving so many kilometres with the defective pump had proven too much. Driving so far without power-steering had obviously damaged the splines on the steering column. Once the power steering pump had been replaced the revitalised brawn brought to force by, we 'operators' and the new pump generated the final demise of those now weaken aluminium splines.

This '**PTI** was no more than a hindrance; our trip was in fact enhanced by the experience. That aside from being stopped at a Police and Veterinary Check Point when all our uncooked meat was confiscated from the on-board fridge. I hope they enjoyed my **F**ood **L**oss **PTI'. (FLPTI)** for dinner that evening. For dinner we tried our utmost to catch a guinea fowl along the way; however, they proved themselves to be much fitter and quicker than either of us or the Disco. Just one was all we needed, from what appeared to be thousands swarming the tracks and bush around us. Sadly, we were to go hungry, in hindsight that was not such a bad thing for a change! At least the Lions would have shared a more flavoursome banquet than our tough old carcasses that day. Landy-Luck kept us from being devoured by the many hungry lions roaming around us.

Our sincere thanks to Land Rover Maun for the good service and hospitality. With their help and that from Landy-Luck we continued our trip making it all the way back to the Western Cape after this **'No Steering' (NSPTI).**

Chapter 5
The Botswana Muffler

Road surfaces around the world come in many guises, from pristine tarred surfaces like many of our major roads, to the pot-holed torments, such as you never saw before. Ranging from giant potholes as found in countries such as Mozambique, to the mud holes of the Congo which, during the rainy season would consume a double decker bus. Betwixt the two there are those lovely dirt/gravel/sand roads, which is why we go out of our way to experience them so far so often. Many miles of backbreaking corrugations can shake the living daylights out of you, your passengers, your vehicle and its contents.

This recalls a **PTI**, with my V8 Disco. Fixer and I were merrily making our way across the Pans of Botswana, suffering a stretch of those bone-shaking corrugations when we sensed a sudden rise in decibels. Oops! The rear silence had taken leave of us, gone away to pastures new, never to be seen again. Tying the tail pipe to the chassis with a length of the ever-present wire, as is found in all Landy tool boxes, we were on our way again after this 'Silencer**PTI**' **(SPTI)**.

Fixing tail pipe with wire

We set off once more, enjoying the new guttural sounding V8. Sadly, there was no one around to be impressed by our new macho tones; apart, that is, from the wildlife which, as usual totally ignored us. Forward and onward we boldly ventured.

Later, in the middle of nowhere, the rest of the exhaust system decided it had tolerated enough of the abuse and cruelty being inflicted upon it. Like the silencer before, it decided a better life was to be found elsewhere. Suddenly, without as much as a 'bye nor leave' it absconded. It ditched us, not just in one piece, but in shreds from manifold to tail pipe. None of it was salvageable so we gathered and loaded up those pieces we could find for later disposal. Decibel levels were now ear-shattering, though I confess, we thought it fantastic at first, until deafness overwhelmed us, making conversation virtually impossible.

Amazingly, with the help of Landy-Luck, about half an hour later we came upon a cross roads, somewhere near the village of Mopipi. There we spotted a couple of petrol pumps with a Tyre and Exhaust Centre right next-door. There was nothing else within sight in any direction. An exhaust mirage perhaps, should we pinch ourselves to be sure? No, we weren't hallucinating it was indeed real. I proved it by walking into one of the solid walls; ouch! Landy-Luck was indeed with us once more.

Inside the scene was one of a very well organised business being carried out. The little guy doing the work greeted us with an assuring and welcoming smile. His overalls were sheathed in weld burns. When I asked if he could repair our exhaust he quickly replied, "I thought you might be in need some work doing as I could hear you coming from way down the road. I've two jobs to finish first, I'll only be about twenty minutes".

True to his word twenty minutes later the Disco was up on the lift. "You need a complete new exhaust system". Of course, it was the expected response as nothing of the original exhaust system was to be seen, apart from the scraps we were carrying in the back of the Disco. "I don't have any in stock" he said.

Not surprising, as there appeared to be very little of anything in stock apart from a few silencers and lengths of pipe. "Don't worry, I'll make a new one for you" he quipped.

What happened next was truly amazing. This little guy looked at the manifolds and removed the shattered remnants of the exhaust flanges. Out came the angle grinder and welder, it was obvious now why there were so many burn holes in his overalls; no goggles or gloves. In just a few minutes he had the manifold brackets ready to accept a new exhaust pipe.

What followed was even more incredible. Using just his hands and arms as a measure, not a tape measure in sight, he estimated the length of each piece of pipe needed then ran off, out of sight, to the store. He soon returned with several lengths of pipe. Each piece he cut to his calculated length with the angle grinder, shaped them with a pipe bender and trimmed the ends. Holding some of this pipe up to the manifold he set to with the welder and hey-presto the first length of new exhaust, with a flange was fixed. He quickly went on to make up the whole length of exhaust pipe. There was just one suitable new silencer in stock, though not for a Land Rover; I suspected it was awaiting a common local Toyota. Inside an hour we had a completely new exhaust system, assembled from scratch and perfectly fitted. What's more it made the V8 sound rather like a young lion roaring. Thankfully it didn't sound like a Toyota.

As the saying goes: "I'd rather push a Land Rover than drive Jap sounding crap".

This 'miracle-man' didn't stop working for a moment, the sweat was pouring off him. When I asked him "How much?" he said, "Go see the man at the desk". Thanking him with a tip of the 11Pula I had in my pocket. The actual bill for the job came to just 10Pula. Did they feel sorry for us, or did they enjoy working on a Landy? That astounding exhaust was still on the Disco when I sold it some two years later.

This was a good **'Muffler PTI' (MPTI)** which I am sure was caused by the many 'corrugations' we had driven over for so long. Just another hurdle to vault along the Landy way, mingled with a hint of operator neglect for not fixing it properly at the time of the tail pipe's initial demise. Upon reflection, I should perhaps have replaced the exhaust many months before and at least checked it over before setting out on this trip. Landy-Luck was once again on our side.

Chapter 6
Namibian Brakes

I do my esteem and reputation no favours in relating this tale. It does however prove the value of friends and how good it is to have them around. They all deserve my CTM many times over for their stalwart efforts.

Overlanding once more in my V8 Disco1 through northern Namibia, we followed the Cunene River from Ruacana in the east to Epupa Falls then further westward to the Skeleton Coast. The Cunene River forms the border between Namibia and Angola.

Namibia   *Angola*

Wild camping on the river bank, sleeping under the stars is magic and difficult to better. That was until I awoke one morning to find strange curving lines and paddle like marks in the sand beside my sleeping bag; may be a large turtle I thought. Moments later a couple of passers-by put me wise. "A crocodile walked very close past you during the night mister"

they were delighted to tell me. I was until that moment, led to believe crocodiles were not to be found in running water. From then on, I slept in my tent.

 I awarded a CTM and a container of milk to that kind man and his young son. They may well have saved me from a later croc fate! Landy-Luck must have sent them to me. They surely saved me from what could possibly have been a **F**atal **C**roc **PTI**. **(FCPTI).**

Croc Detectors

We went on to negotiate the wonderful Van Zyls Pass, a notorious 'one way' trail in northern Namibia. The Pass is named after Ben Van Zyl, who was once a commissioner In Koakoland. In 1965 he created a way across the Baynes Mountain country. With the help of twenty local Himba people, using just pickaxes, shovels and crowbars he created the track by following a long existing wildlife and cattle trail. It has since been popularised by the many 'thrill-seeking' over-landers. Up many steep climbs and down even steeper drops to Marienfluss plain, on our way toward the Skeleton Coast, passing the famed Red Drum marker. The drum is fitted with a telephone, though not connected to any phone system; it's there as a 'bridge point' and for fun.

Having made it to the plain it is customary to sign a stone adding it to the cairn built by previous 'trekkers' on wheels; or on foot as Ms.Titia du Plessis who found four wheels just too scary. She wrote on her stone "I may be scared, but not lazy, I walked the pass". Quite some walk, she deserves one of my CTMs.

Van Zyls maid road

It would be great to make the return trip; in a Landy that is, not on foot! Not only would that be classed 'extreme' but certainly not advisable, or permitted, as it would be hazardous to those making their way in the correct East to West route.

From Marienfluss we made our way back toward the Cunene river and the Angolan border. By the riverside we met families that had been torn apart by the 27-year war of independence from the former South West Africa. Namibia became so named in 1990 by the then SA President F W de Klerk, after the war when independence was granted. We were fascinated to hear their loud clear voices chatting away over the mighty river; no cell phones or I-pads for them. I hope the day will come when those families and friends can be once again re-united.

We camped for a night near the river at a state-run campsite near Otjinhungwa, allegedly the most northern campsite in Namibia. I slept out in my sleeping bag, with just a mozzie net between me and the brilliantly clear stars. I did check that the river was too far away for another 'croc' incident.

The following morning, I discovered a box of cheap white wine in my on-board fridge had leaked; what a mess!

Everything was floating in a mixture of wine and icy water thawed out by the wine. We emptied the fridge and poured the 'fluid' into a couple of empty two litre milk containers we happened to have with us. While thinking of the best way to dispose of this 'cocktail' Landy-Luck arrived, in the form of the site attendant doing his rounds on his bicycle. We were the only campers on site, so he made a bee line for us for a chat and see if perhaps we may have something for him. I offered him the containers of our 'special brew', which he accepted with much gratitude, having first removed a top to sniff the contents.

Off he went with his bicycle well loaded, but only as far as the ablutions block. We continued to breakfast, decamp and load up our Landys ready to depart which took well over an hour.

When we left to make our way to the Skeleton Coast the happy chappie was still in the toilet enjoying his free **W**ine **C**ocktail **PTI (WCPTI)**.

At times along this coast it is almost impossible to see through the rolling mist. The coastline is known locally as the largest ship's graveyard. As the cold 'in shore' air rolls off the Atlantic Ocean it meets the very hot Namibian desert 'off shore' air creating a dense mist. Vision is wiped out and any sense of direction or location becomes confused - hence the wrecks.

Many ships have come to grief over the years, caught in that blinding mist; more so during the days prior to GPS.

We continued our way leisurely, enjoying the notorious Skeleton Coast. The last thing on my mind, while taking a close look at one of the many wrecks, was of becoming interred in this marine graveyard.

It was time to leave but the Disco wouldn't budge, she was jammed solid, having sunken up to her axles. Once more I had arrived at that popular location now well known as 'Gottenstuk'

No problem we thought, after all there were six of us. Richard ('The Animal'.) had his Land Rover 110, the 'Workhorse,' fitted with a winch, sand ladders and every imaginable piece of gear! We winched, laddered, pushed, pulled, shoved, shovelled, grunted, sweated and swore, all to no avail – she wouldn't budge from Gottenstuk. Workhorse was set up as anchor point for winching. Obviously, we were all very anxious. Workhorse was parked up on terra ferma as far away as the joint lengths of winch cable, ropes and strops we had with us allowed. Had the Disco had been facing in the right direction we could have connected both winches giving the added benefit of more distance giving even lower gearing and more power to our efforts.

My Gottenstuk PTI (GPTI)

We couldn't afford to have Workhorse sink into the same quandary as my Disco. With the six of us pushing, combined with high revving, sand-laddering, shovelling, winching, plus a good dose of the essential 'verbal' input she moved, but only just, she was skidding along. Her wheels refused to turn. Eventually with oodles of Landy-Luck we managed to drag, push and shove the Disco out sledge-like. I kept trying to turn the steering wheel, in the hope of gaining some traction, but the steering was jammed solid. How I didn't manage to break a half-shaft, steering rod or even worse I don't know.

It had now turned into a serious 'sh*1*t or bust' situation; the tide was rising softening the sand surface. Fortunately, our combined efforts generated enough 'oomph' to become 'unstuck' at last.

Proud of our recovery skills we soon realised why the wheels wouldn't turn. On and under the sandy surface was a mass of loose, multi sized pebbles, many just of the right size to lodge between the spokes of all four wheels. No problem I thought, just remove the rocks and off we go. Rocks removed and – oops!! – One wheel broken. *(Lesson: Forget about alloy wheels for overlanding. Steel wolf wheels for me from now on.)* The broken wheel was not a major issue as between us we had four spares on board. While we were changing the broken front wheel, we noticed there was no brake caliper. A further check revealed that another rear caliper had met with the same demise. I recall saying "Oh dear", or something like that. 'Missing' was not perhaps the precise term to describe the demise as the calipers were there but crushed to smithereens and being dragged along by the now screwed-up brake pipes.

Another challenge was yet to be met and overcome.

Here we are in a restricted area and the gates close at 7.30pm. This is a diamond mining area and for some reason the authorities get somewhat touchy should you overstay your welcome. It's now turned 7pm and there's some distance to cover between us and the exit gate. To save time we towed the brakeless Disco, getting to the gate just in time, or maybe a tad late. I explained to the guard greeting us at the gate that we had suffered a minor breakdown along the way. I admit not being totally honest as to the whereabouts or circumstances, as after the recovery I discovered it is forbidden to drive on the beach where we were. Please accept my apologies; I would not have gone there had I known beforehand. *(Lesson: carry out more research before setting out).*

We spent considerable time with the guard as he related the history of the Skeleton Coast, its many wrecks, minerals, gems, rocks, and mines; also, of the failed oil drilling enterprise.

He was in his element. We avoided any talk of the sad Disco parked outside. It was now late, and we were on our way, worn out and 'brakeless' to rest up overnight.

Feeling refreshed after a good night's sleep, decisions had to be made. Fortunately, I had with me a list of various African Landy contacts that friend Schalk Burger had given me.

From his list I called up Juan Strauss near Windhoek, some 600km away. *(My remark about 'water music' didn't strike a chord).* Before I finished asking Juan if he had any brake calipers for a '96 Disco V8 he re-joined with "Yes, and you will also need pads and brake pipes". Giving him our location, he retorted without hesitation – "Go to the Star Café in Henties Bay, George will be there with your parts at 12:30 tomorrow". We agreed the price and finished off with Landy chat and many thanks. Landy-Luck played her part once again!

Henties Bay was some 300km away, so Fixer and I set to making the Disco mobile. Fortunately, we had two pairs of mole grips with us; see we are not just 'hammer and screwdriver' Landy mechanics. Fixer had a good idea; he folded the two broken brake pipes open ends over, clamped each with the mole grips, sealing them off. We topped up the brake fluid and bled the brakes that we had left and 'hey presto' we were mobile once again with some sort of braking power.

With just front offside and rear nearside brakes straight line braking was difficult, so we kept to the slower dirt roads, avoiding traffic as much as possible. That would have been our preference anyhow.

Progress was steady, though at times obstructed, at one point having to wait whilst a cow was slaughtered Halal style in the road in front of us. Maybe they were rustlers? For us it was a **'HaLal' PTI (HLPTI)**

Along the way we encountered a couple of enjoyable **PTI**s when we came across two Land Rover wrecks, 'parked up' since the war with Angola.

We had to take a close look of course, estimating in our heads how long it would take to get them back 'up and running'; it could be a very long **R**eno **PTI (RPTI).**

We made frequent brake checks to make sure we could stop if necessary. On one such check, I footed the brake pedal expecting to come to a slow down when the pedal floored with no reaction or resistance whatsoever. Rapidly changing down through the gears, the Disco eventually came to a halt. One of the mole grips had fallen off a brake pipe draining the brake fluid. We carried on brakeless.

It may take a wee while to get these back on their wheels (RPTI)

Driving into Henties Bay that afternoon we found the Star Café. The kind lady there said as I walked in, before I uttered a sound, "My brother George is expecting you at twelve thirty tomorrow. He will have the parts you need with him".

Then George's very kind sister, as she turned out to be, made a phone call arranging free accommodation for us in the beautiful Henties bay. That night we dined and slept in the comfort of a four bedroomed house with all facilities imaginable. There was even a garage high enough to take the Disco complete with its loaded roof-rack. Why didn't we stay longer, we'd hardly used the Braai? I don't have room in my garage for my Landy, even without a roof-rack.

Next day, as promised, at 12:30 precisely, George was at the Star Cafe with the box of parts in his arms. I paid him the price agreed with Juan. George directed us in the direction of a garage in town. "They are expecting you" he said, then off he went to carry on his business as the local butcher. We had in fact already visited that very garage earlier that morning, as a few minor jobs required attention; one of which involved removing the front nearside wheel. The missing front caliper must have been clear to see but they said nothing. I was sure they were expecting us to call in the next day to fix the brakes.

We went back to the garage, once we had the parts, for the brakes to be repaired. The work was carried out most professionally and efficiently.

Once again, we were happily mobile to continue our amazing travels. This **'R**ock **W**recker **PTI' (RWPTI)** was caused by 'operator *(me!)* senselessness'.

> When Land Rover owners die, they go straight to Heaven.
> As they have had so much "Hell on earth"

So untrue, as we all know; perhaps a **H**eavenly **PTI (HPTI)** with the help of loads of Landy-Luck.

Thank you once again Land Rover for taking us 'so far by far', and to all the good friends there to help me; Richard (The Animal), Monique, Byorn and Sven; not forgetting the other Richard (Fixer).

Just another chapter of life's wonderful Landy 'Experiences'. Well-earned CTMs to all involved.

With a Landy there are always friends when you need them together with a lot of Landy-Luck close by.

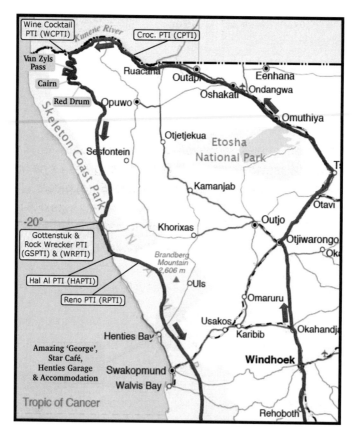

Chapter 7
Kalahari Clutch

Thirteen 'mates' with a Kalahari dream drove their
Landys for fun in Botswana.

Most of us!

The Land Rovers in the party consisted of:-
DiscoV8 a Defender110 300Tdi a Defender Td5,
Defender Td5 Twin Cab and a LR90 Tdi Soft Top.

We made pleasurable and **PTI** free progress over the 1,300km from Greyton to Tsabong which is just over the border into Botswana. That is except for one good friend Stuart, who due to commitments back home was unable to leave at the same time as the rest of us.

We arrived at Tsabong village to find a very welcoming small shop and fuel pumps which we made very good use of. After topping up our tanks, bellies and fridges we went just a little way down the road to Berrybush Accommodation.

We were made to feel very welcome at Berrybush, a most friendly, charming and delightful place to stay. Just as we had settled in our friend Stuart arrived in his Defender Td5.

His delayed arrival hardly registered with us, in fact, his timing couldn't have been better as all was ready for him, the braai was warming up and the vino was breathing, almost ready to pour. Stuart was concerned about the clutch in his Td5 which was slipping. Of course, this was like music to our ever listening and enthusiastic Land-Rovering ears! A **PTI** challenge delivered right into our laps. Was Landy-Luck thinking of us once again, though I'm sure Stuart didn't see it quite that way. Action was needed to 'fix' his clutch in the Kalahari Desert. This was too good a challenge to turn down.

First things first, at least by our reckoning, it was back down to the petrol pumps to find out where the nearest Land Rover parts supplier might be. Neither the garage nor the shop staff had any idea where we might source the needed parts.

What to do next?

Just then, as I was about to consult Schalk's 'Landy List,' Landy-Luck pulled up at the pumps in a new Defender 110 with 'UN' logos on the front doors. It was manned by two smartly attired military officers looking for fuel. I asked if they could help with the details of any local Land Rover parts supplier. "Sorry" was the swift but cordial reply "we are not from around here". Landy-Luck once more came to our aide when the officer in the front passenger seat said – "hang on, we just collected this Land Rover from the main dealer in Gaborone".

Well, that's some 500km or more away from Tsabong. He went on to say, "Look I just found this tub of sweets left here in the Landy for us by the dealer". This good bit of Landy marketing had the dealership full details on the lid. Once again, as I've said, when in a state of **PTI** someone nearly always turns up.

It's now 4:55pm, the shop and fuel station were about to close. I called the phone number on the lid as quickly as I could to be answered by a most helpful responsive guy, whose name sadly I don't now recall. I explained our need for a clutch plate for a TD5. He asked for the VIN number, which Stuart had to hand, immediately he confirmed the parts were in stock.

With the price agreed, I paid by card over the phone.

He asked where we were, I told him Tsabong. Before I could utter further syllable, he retorted, "The parts will be in Tsabong by 8:30 tomorrow morning". When asked whereabouts he swiftly replied - "there is a small shop there with two fuel pumps outside. They will be in the shop ready for you". That was right where I was standing at that moment; Gaborone is some 500km away! A small country is Africa! Do Landys frequently break down in Tsabong I asked myself?

I don't know how it happened, but African Express couriers had delivered the parcel before 8am when I was at the shop the next morning. Landy-Luck had been busy on our behalf. The efforts of both Land Rover Gaborone and African Express earn each a well-deserved CTM.

Not expecting to be faced with the challenge of carrying out the repair quite so soon or expecting to get the parts in such a short time we had to plan for 'Bush Repairs'. Where do we find a 'Four Post Lift' or 'Pit' so the gear box could be removed the 'proper way' from below? None around, so some inventive thinking and a compromise were called for. Four spare wheels were strategically sited on the ground. Stuart's Defender was driven up onto them, one wheel onto each tyre, giving enough ground clearance for us to crawl underneath; if only to get covered in grease and sand. This gave us enough space to remove the cross member allowing a little more access and work space.

No way could we safely remove the gearbox from below; we didn't want to bury Stuart's fine machine in the Kalahari sand just yet as she was the youngest of the posse. Fixer came up with an idea to remove the gearbox from above, inside the cabin, which sounded easy enough at first. The cubby box, gear lever and front seats were removed, well that was simple enough. The floor panels were removed as was the front of the centre box with no problem. The gearbox was exposed, at least in part! The only problem being the supporting bar across the front under the cubby box; not a nut or bolt in sight, it is welded in place.

After much consultation and deliberation Stuart reluctantly consented to surgery. The hacksaw was summoned; soon the operation was underway.

At it from above and below

Happily, it was a success; Brave Stuart having not taken any anaesthetic of any kind soon recovered. There was still much to be done from both above and below, such as removing the hand brake cable and drum and the clutch slave cylinder. The prop shafts were disconnected and gear box securing bolts removed. Many other less obvious items had to be tended to, such as the battery made safe and the like. There were many of us; the camaraderie was great, all was going well.

Now to remove the gearbox. Up to this moment our 'grey matter' had not been stretched too far in this direction.

Fixer again came up with an idea; he got a broom from Berrybush. The handle went into the cab above the gear box from side to side; a couple of ratchet straps were wrapped around the gearbox and the broom handle and tightened. The 'many hands' were brought into action, The Animal scored well here; together we lifted the broom handle with gear box attached. It wasn't quite so easy moving it sideways out of the cab, but success came with care. *(Sorry no images of these stages as all hands were very busy.)*

What followed I am sure was a routine procedure, removing and replacing a clutch plate. Of course, there was no alignment tool for the spigot shaft. No worries, we did have a length of pipe, it wasn't the right diameter; the difference we made up with insulating tape.

Once the new clutch was fitted the gearbox had to go back into the Landy. 'Bring back the broom', it took a while, but all went well. The Bush made Alignment Tool performed well. I still have it ready, willing and able for more service.

Have we been fixing a Landy?

Much to Stuart's relief his Landy worked well from then on. It was suggested to us later, that an adjustment on the Td5 pedal box could have cured the problem. Yes, there is an adjustment; but in this case it was not appropriate as there was the required 140mm of travel on the clutch pedal; as we learnt on our return to Greyton.

As ten Chinese standing around a broken light bulb once explained, "Many hands make light work"

We spent a couple more pleasant days at Berrybush after the **K**alahari **C**lutch **PTI. (KCPTI)**. CTMs all round, especially for Stuart.

It was a splendid display of Landy teamwork.

Chapter 8
Chainsaw Massage

Back home in England, after much thinking, planning and procrastinating, I finally decided what I would like to do in Boudie. To South Africa I would go, though not by any easy route, if there be such a thing? I gathered together a willing team and vehicles. Routes were compiled, and we continued to cogitate and ruminate.

The team was to be John and Roz Onions, friends of many years. They would drive their, well prepared and overland ready, Discovery1, a good specimen in excellent condition.

We named her Comarra; after another of Boudies' daughters. Richard Box (Fixer), an 'offroad' friend and neighbour well steeped into the world of Landy Living, would drive my Discovery1, Tasca; yet to be kitted out.

The crew, as originally planned

I would be partnered in Boudie by enthusiastic friend Bronnie (Paps), who had flown over from South Africa to join the team. Our mascot Bilko would of course also be on board.

There was much to be done; the list was long.

Boudie needed more attention to make her fit for such an exciting adventure; at least that's what I imagined! I fitted a 'Turner Head' enabling us to use leaded or unleaded petrol; an important consideration when traversing different countries and continents. It also helps improve performance, and economy. Not that I have any computed results to quote from, just pure gut feeling based on past and present experience, along with a degree of 'wallet watching'. The rear tub was fitted out with a plywood raised floor making room to stow ammo boxes underneath with tents, cool box and loads more above. I built in a small 'secret' compartment which later proved very handy, as did the safe I fitted under the driver's seat. The interior of the tub was fitted with a cage for security as canvass is easily accessed by wandering inquisitive hands.

Our chosen route would take us via Dover Port by ferry to Calais and onwards south through France to Italy. From there by ferry from Genoa, via the Mediterranean to Tunis then drive across Tunisia into Algeria. Then we would have a great time crossing the Sahara Desert into Niger on into Nigeria and Cameroon. Later we would hit the Congo for a 'mud fix', *(the main reason for choosing this route)* before continuing via Zambia into Malawi where we planned to visit an orphanage in Lilongwe. The last leg would be a relatively easy drive to my African home in the Western Cape, through Zimbabwe and Botswana; a total of fourteen countries.

We mapped out and agreed the route. Carnets and Visas were arranged, the Land Rovers kitted out and loaded to the gunnels. From experience, I advise a thorough survey of exactly what you need to take with you. We, of course, took far too much 'gear' based upon advice from 'experts', friends, magazines and on a 'just in case' scenario. Less is better, believe me, as we later learnt the hard way!

Before a wheel turned our first **PTI** of the trip befell us when one of John's feet got into a close relationship with a chain saw. Departure was delayed while his foot was fixed, and he recovered from this **'C**hain **S**aw **M**assage' **(CSPTI)**. *(Not quite a 'Chainsaw Massacre')*. Thankfully his injury turned out to be not as bad as at first feared.

Excitement was building as healing progressed well. John, a fit, healthy outdoor and hardworking friend, sadly out of the blue suddenly became very sick. This peaked with the removal of his gall-bladder. We waited for him to recover from the operation but, not surprisingly, his doctor advised against travelling as a result of his **G**all-**B**ladder **PTI** **(GB-PTI)'**.

Chapter 9
Dover Delayed Boarding

I decided not to give up now that we were reduced to two Landys, Boudie and Tasca. 'Paps' was on a three-month UK visa, the delay meant the sand in her egg timer was now running low, and the pressure to be on the way was rising. Meanwhile Tasca was kitted out with a roof rack and a roof top tent, a Solar system and all the usual camping, and cooking gear along with other living bits and bobs. A 40L fridge was installed and a winch fitted. We left for Dover, regrettably without John and Roz or Comarra. The first night's stopover we spent camping in the grounds of beautiful Providence House and grounds in Lenham village in Kent. Thanks to Richard and Leelee Kock, good friends of Pap's, for inviting us to rest up overnight. After pitching camp, we meandered down to the nearby 1670 Kings Head pub where we imbibed in a few bevies of a local brew, which fermented plenty of friendly banter. Back at camp we had a great BBQ, with again more liquid 'chatter fuel' which had us all jawing and jesting 'till sleep overtook us with dreams of what lay ahead.

Next morning, we packed up and set off for the port of Dover to catch the ferry to Calais. The queue was long and slow; the situation became further aggravated when a customs officer spotted the jerry can I had fitted onto Boudie's front fender. Pleasant talk, a handshake and smiles avoided a more serious **PTI**. Of course, Landy-Luck helped smooth things over. Not the safest place to carry a jerry can full of petrol, though at this time it was empty, purposely so, until reaching a source of less expensive fuel.

Following this **'D**elayed **B**oarding**' PTI. (DBPTI)** we were on our way to Calais; all was 'ship-shape and Bristol fashion'.

A CTM to Brittany Ferries, it was an excellent crossing in every way.

Boudie and Tasca travelled well on their first sea crossing. Until now Boudie had travelled by road and air, being dropped off from helicopters during her earlier life serving with the British Military. It was good to find she did in fact also have good 'Sea Legs', as indeed did Tasca.

Chapter 10
Bubbly PTIs

Landy-Luck brought us to the Epernay Champagne region for our first night's French camping. We blended in with the locals who were 'letting their hair down' during their annual 'Champagne Festival'. There are around 900 champagne caves nearby in the Marne region. Oh dear, did I sense self-inflicted **PTI**s coming on? We manage to easily down several glasses of the most agreeable bubbly. There was so much to see and much compulsory sampling we had to take in. This was one very pleasant case of **PTI** in champagne glasses. Many hiccupping thanks go to Landy-Luck for these '**B**ubbly' **PTI**s. **(BPTI)**.

Here Paps was in her 'champagne heaven'. We spent a day in Epernay, walking the Avenue de Champagne where the big names all had a presence. It was here that Paps bumped into an old friend of hers by the name of Dom.

Mr. Dom Perignon seemed quite a star. Paps has known Dom for years but this was the first time the two met face to face. Until now they had only ever chatted by the glass.

It was Dom who told Paps that 'a meal without wine is

Paps meets Dom

like a day without sunshine'; a message passed on, embraced and heartily adopted by all. Dom was unable to join us on an incredible 18km tour of a champagne cave nearby at Mercier. All the way we were taken under amazing brick arches, all some thirty metres under ground, built in 1889, when 280,000 tonnes of chalk stone was excavated. This was just one of the nine hundred such caves we were told could be found in the region; yet more '**BPTIs**' were sipped. There are some three thousand champagne vineyards in the area so the strong likelihood of even more '**BPTIs**' loomed.

We had to move on. Sadly, I was discouraged from filling Boudie's on-board 40Litre water tank with bubbles before leaving. So off we went on our way, enjoying the scenery, cuisine and the wonderful wines and eats along the way.

I'm sure Landy-Luck played her part in dissuading me from loading bubbles on board!

Wherever Boudie set wheel in France, and everywhere else she showed herself, she was much admired by all around her. Land Rover you are missing a wonderful marketing opportunity, 'that retro look and the character'? If just one percent of those coveting Boudie translated that desire into a purchase of a borne-again look alike, there would be a tidal wave of demand for such treasures. What about all those other countries around the world now denied a robust, basic, hard-working, unbreakable, simple to fix, all-terrain workhorse. Isn't that what Land Rover should be all-about since the line drawing on the beach in Wales all those years ago?

Why Land Rover have you chosen to cease production of the ubiquitous, versatile immensely popular Lightweight and Defender? Forget the military, there's a market there for these versatile, un-gizmo'd trouble free, go anywhere 4x4's.

Chapter 11

Burst Pipe

The French Pyrenees proved an exciting and a healthy challenge for Boudie. It was as if we were in heaven forging through the glorious countryside. However, I was getting grief from Paps, complaining about the heat rising from the cab floor. "I can't imagine what it's going to be like when we go through the Sahara" she quipped. I fear I made things worse by explaining the exhaust pipe passed under the passenger seat, and yes, it will get much warmer, once we are in the Sahara Desert. I heated the atmosphere in the cab even more by muttering about the space taken up in the rear tub by her 'Wells Fargo safe' style camera case. Apart from that Boudie and Paps were having a wonderful time negotiating those amazing passes.

The French Pyrenees are so beautiful, well most of the time that is. They happened to be along my chosen route from the UK to South Africa. Paps, by now had fallen in love with Boudie, driving her as if they had been partners for years. Driving through the quiet 'shuttered' villages, no cars or motorbikes, no people, no kids, just silence and beautiful rolling countryside all around. Setting up camp for a night at Janzet, Fixer had an issue with a burst water pipe on Tasca.

This was no problem for him. Quickly up with the bonnet, he found it to be a heater pipe leaking. Would you believe it we found a replacement pipe amongst the plethora of 'bits' we had on board; and there I am continually rabbiting on about our being 'overloaded'. After about half an hour with the pipe repaired and bonnet down Tasca was whole once more; QED. Fixer was rather greasy, or should I say 'Landy-Tinted', but successfully cured this **'Burst Pipe PTI' (BPPTI).**

We set off next morning to tackle the midi Pyrenees Mountains. The views, flora and fauna were wonderful. At lunch time, on a Sunday, we decided to stop at what looked like a charming, peaceful café for a bite of lunch. We were abruptly refused entry by the proprietor with a very firm, and rather rude "ferme" at us as we entered; at least I knew what ferme meant!

Was it us or our Land Rovers they took exception to? However, this didn't dampen our enthusiasm for the area with those quaint, quiet villages and our love of the mountain passes we were criss-crossing, and our desire for more French cuisine.

Perhaps it may have been different had we been driving a Renault or Citroen.

Chapter 12
The French Disconnection

Our enthusiasm was soon to be dented a little later while crossing a pass in the Pyrenees. Suddenly, without warning it became impossible to shift Boudie into any gear other than first or second, despite attempts at double-declutching and the application of brute force.

Fixer' and I spent time lying under Boudie at the roadside attempting to get at the gearbox. Our sole achievement was to get very 'Landy-Tinted', which of course is 'par for the course' as every Land Rover has oil underneath; if not, there's none in it. This was one of the very few times that Landy-Luck has not sent another Landy along to help.

Onwards we very slowly went, fortunately the Fairey overdrive gave a little more momentum in the two gears that were left. I was perhaps extra cautious as I didn't want to ruin the gearbox, blow the new Turner head, or even worse. I did have to remind the concerned Paps that this was not a breakdown, just a case of **P**rogress being **T**emporarily **S**lowed through a deceleration of forward motion.

So where do you find a Land Rover garage in France during their holiday month of August, when everywhere is closed?

We had planned to visit an uncle of Pap's living in Montferrier-sur-Lez, further ahead in the South of France. Just then Landy-Luck stepped in when, at that very moment, uncle Ruxton called Paps on her cell phone to find out when we would be arriving at his home. He was able to tell Paps of a Land Rover workshop in the town of Rodez, some 60km away.

'Ethel', our faithful GPS, was put into action, set for Rodez and off we slowly progressed. Along the way we stumbled upon a family run garage in a small village where we met four wonderful French guys in the workshop. They were extremely friendly and helpful. Willingly they would have set to find and fix the problem but securing parts would have been more than difficult for them during the annual holiday. They called up the Land Rover garage we were en route to in Rodez. Finding there was someone on site they explained our plight and booked us into the Hotel Bastide in Rodez for the night. Happy and feeling upbeat off we went, albeit at a snail's pace, on our way to Rodez. For their camaraderie and willingness, they gain one of my Camel Trophies.

Next morning, as agreed, we went to the garage in Rodez to be pleasantly surprised by the friendly welcome from manager Fernand, engineer Carlos, and P.A. Cathy Bourdillat. They were 'keeping a watchful eye' on the place, over the holiday period. Arrangements were made to bring Boudie to them, once we had settled into the recommended local Camp de Layoule, just outside town. This was to be our home for the next week or so.

Once settled into the campsite Fixer and I set about stripping Boudie making her ready for her operation.

The seats were taken out, floor panels, transmission tunnel, gear lever and box cover removed, ever hopeful of finding the cause of the problem. But no, we couldn't, even with frequent phone calls to Bryn our Landy guru in the UK. We did manage to check the gear selectors which we found to be in fine working order. Tasca then towed Boudie to the garage where she was rested up in comfort awaiting the diagnosis and operation as soon as the crew returned from holiday.

Meanwhile our time was split between our tents and up and down the many steps to the Ville de Rodez where there were many sites and 'tastes' to be enjoyed.

We hired a car to explore the local area. Indeed, it was a bonus as there was so much to see and do in the region.

It's now the 31st August and everyone is back to work. Carlos quickly set to work on Boudie, as suspected, a broken synchro on third gear was the cause of this **PTI**.

Fixing Boudie's gearbox

Top marks and a CTM to 'Allmakes' for sending a replacement overnight from the UK.

Very soon the job was done, and all was working well. Fernand then made out the invoice. Before handing it to me he looked it over and decided it was just too much. Several phone calls later he tore it up and charged a much lesser amount. Thanks go to you Fernand, Carlos, Cathy and all at Land Rover Rodez for a giving us a great 'Land Rover Experience'.

I won't mention that they also sell and look after contrivances under the Volvo banner!

All was rounded off in the garage by joining in with all the staff with a glass of champagne. We thought at first the party was in our honour; but no, we had just latched on to a leaving party for one of the office staff. Whatever, it was a great 'send-off'.

Team Rodez

Thank you all again at Car Services, Rodez; Land Rover should be proud of you. A CTM to each for your service, help and friendliness.

The Team at Rodez turned this hiccup into a most enjoyable week of **F**rench **D**isconnection **PTI (FDPTI)** & '**S**ynchro' **& C**hampagne **PTI (S&C PTI)**

Thank you all, and of course uncle Ruxton and Land-Luck for your help.

Chapter 13
Monaco Grand Prix

Back at the campsite we replaced the panels and the other parts we had earlier stripped out in readiness for the synchro repair and reloaded all our paraphernalia. I purchased a roll of Foil Bubble Insulation which Fixer and I lined Boudie's cabin with to help combat the heat, which was becoming more annoying as the outside temperatures rose. This caused only a little bit of an Insulating **PTI. (IPTI)**

Moving on we uploaded many pleasant memories and found some brilliant French campsites as we journeyed along the Riviera coast. The only **PTI**s experienced were of the self-inflicted self-indulgent kind.

Some trivial **PTI**s were created by 'frustrations' caused by the French holidays and a ferry delay. The synchro breakdown, on its own, under normal circumstances, would merely have been a 'hiccup', though it was a bonus to have spent more time than planned around Rodez. The walks, cafes, the coffee avec 'petite pain au chocolate' and 'tarte au pomme', mingled with the views and ambiance, made it all most agreeable. We were looking forward to more **PTI**s in that lovely region of France; unfortunately, it was not to be.

CTMs all round on this occasion of Land Rover 'Experience'. Land Rover and their agents and various parts suppliers, once again, kept us going '4x4 by Far'.

We were happy to be motoring on our way once more. The delay meant changing our pre-booked ferry ticket to a later sailing than originally booked via Genoa to Tunis. The rest of the trip through France, Monaco and Italy went without any serious impediment.

I'll not forget crossing the Millau Valley over the Millau Bridge spanning the River Tarn in the valley. It is the world's tallest bridge, with one mast reaching a height of 343 meters. Designed by the English architect Sir Norman Foster, it is ranked as one of the greatest engineering achievements of all time.

Landy-Luck insisted we took our Landys into Monaco for Boudie and Tasca to complete

Millau Bridge

a part lap of the Monaco F1 Grand Prix circuit. Whilst the lap times were not good enough to qualify, they both enjoyed their 'experience' of this **M**onaco **GP PTI (MGPPTI.)**

We thoroughly enjoyed our time in France during the 'French Disconnection' experience at Rodez. After that little distraction we carried on **PTI** free through the South of France. Passing through enchanting places such as Cassis, *(chocolate heaven),* St. Tropez, Le Muy, Nice and Marseilles to a campsite near Genoa. We pitched our tents at a site in Savona overlooking the Mediterranean, where we spent our last night in Europe. It had been raining hard for the previous couple of days. While we imbibed at the wonderful café on site, our tent got flooded and our laundry, which I had just washed and ironed, got a second thorough rinsing. We packed it up wet, along with wet tents for an early morning departure after experiencing a well **L**aundered **PTI (LPTI)?**

Boarding the ferry for Tunisia was trouble free, though as we learnt from recent experiences, much patience was a necessary ingredient. Getting to the ferry was rather confusing as the signage, as we drove into the port, comprised of one sign pointing east and another pointing west both indicating 'To the Ferry'. Border control presented a further challenge as the Polizia insisted the entrance door be kept closed, but there wasn't a handle on the outside. It took us a while to gain entry and complete our transit forms. By banging on the door to attract attention, we eventually gained entry, 'formed up' and boarded the ferry, despite the **P**olizia **D**oor **PTI (PDPTI)**.

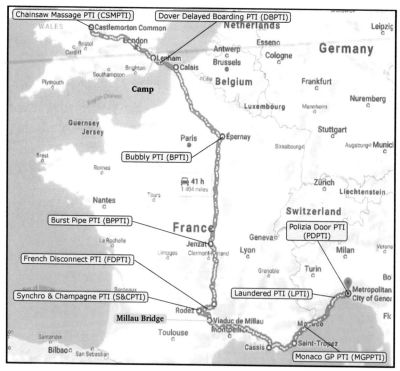

Chapter 14
Tunisian 'Salt Pan'

The ferry crossing was good in every way and off-loading in Tunis was trouble free. Progress was good once we very slowly cleared customs hassle free. This was an easy chapter in our on-going 'border control' apprenticeship programme.

As we journeyed our way through Tunisia towards our next target, Algeria, it was almost **PTI** free.

Finding a campsite near the coast proved challenging, there just aren't any, so we enjoyed a night in luxury in the Hotel Topkapi-Beach at the seaside town of Hammamet. (*To be recommended, though sadly later to be targeted by terrorists*). While checking in, we were warned that alcohol was forbidden by religion and by law. Why ever did they say that as the bar and restaurant were packed with revellers imbibing in a dram or three and having a riotous time. We soon 'liquefied' into the friendly and happy scene.

Next day, after exploring the wonderful coastline as far south as Sousse, still hoping to find a camp site, without success, we ventured inland. We ended up wild camping at a dot of a place called Megda in desert surroundings. Strange isn't it, no matter where you are and how peaceful you think the site you've found may be, someone manages to come along. Sure enough, at around 5am, as we were early rising about to breakfast and decamp, a poncho attired nomadic horseman rides by on a white horse. Pleasantly passing the time of day, he about-turned and trotted back to wherever it was he came from, probably to report to the village elders about the squatters in the neighbourhood.

Wild camping at Megda

We were now heading toward Algeria, via towns such as Tozeur and Naftah, to the Tunisian-Algerian border at Hazoua.

Any **PTI**s enjoyed in Tunisia were self-inflicted through 'playing in the sand', enjoying Saharan 'molehills' along with sightseeing, all of which we enjoyed at will and in abundance. All were **F**un **PTI (FPTI)**, though perhaps not quite the sort of activity to put the Landys through with such a long trek ahead.

One challenging **PTI** came to pass as we neared the town of Tozeur. **P**rogress became **T**ruly **I**mpeded as the smooth desert sand turned into a salt pan. Moisture was invisible under the hard crust of sand. The heavily loaded Tasca sank to her diffs, arriving at 'Gottenstuk' once again. Swift action was called for. Our best efforts with the kinetic rope didn't work.

Boudie wasn't heavy enough, she was jettisoned towards the stuck Tasca at each attempt. It was as if Tasca was playing yo-yo with Boudie recoiling her at each attempt. Surprisingly there was no one anywhere in sight; and didn't I say someone always turned up to help.

We couldn't afford to have both Landys suffer a 'Gottenstuk' **PTI,** so resorting to Boudie's winch, we slowly and luckily made the recovery. Thank you, Landy-Luck, for eventually showing

Boudie recovering Tasca

up to make the recovery successful. This is the one time the overloaded Boudie was of benefit, making her a heavy anchor point.

Talk about David and Goliath, little Boudie, performed amazingly in recovering, the even more heavily overloaded Tasca. Looking back, it was an enjoyable **Salt Pan PTI (SPPTI).**

It was almost impossible, to detect those areas of 'moist' salt pans until you arrive at 'Gottenstuk'. We later discovered we were at the edge of a large salt pan known as Chott el Jerid, some 20km wide by 250km long. This Pan was one of the many film locations used for the Star Wars films. I wonder how the film crews managed?

The BF Goodrich 'AT' tyres fitted to Tasca, while great in most situations are not good in the hot and soft midday sun drenched sand. The tread digs in, even though we had deflated for max effect. The Michelin MZ fitted to Boudie were not much better. From past 'rallying' experiences I find the less aggressive Michelin MXC to be better in the sand. Why didn't I fit them?

It was now I realised, we were overloaded with all the gear we packed for our trip.

I should have learnt from the Englishman Robert L Jefferson, who back in 1907, with a South African friend, Frank Connock, made the very first African overland venture by motorised transport.

The pair drove a single cylinder 8hp Rover car, from Durban to Cape Town via Johannesburg, taking sixteen days to complete the trip. What were the roads or tracks, if any, like in those days? He purposely chose the

Single cylinder 8hp Rover

lightest car available at the time, with the least space to carry 'unnecessary' clutter. His entire 'kit' was just a tool box fitted low under the floor. Food and drinks were obtained as required along the way.

His thinking was that a light vehicle could easily be pushed, pulled or lifted out of any situation when necessary.

When stuck, with the help of a few locals the Rover could be lifted and carried. Sound advice, which I now attempt to follow. 'Landy-Luck' was around all those years ago; maybe it was 'Rover-Luck' in those pre Landy times! These days we take the largest vehicle possible packed to the gunnels; but then we do so like our home comforts and bling!

Two years previously Jefferson achieved another first by driving the same car from Coventry in the UK overland to Constantinople in Turkey. I wonder, is this when a 'Rover' first became a 'Land Rover'?

The town of Tozeur, near the Algerian border, created a few **PTI**s, each one self-imposed; brought about by the friendliness of the people, the cafes, the sights and the campsite. Most of these **PTI**s went under the 'Leisure' heading. They were nothing to do with Land Rover, just simple pure unadulterated merriment. I'm sure Landy-Luck played her part in presenting us with these **Leisure PTI (LPTI)**

The region is famous for its dates, the edible ones that is. Our arrival coincided with the date harvesting time, which unfortunately attracts swarms of winged visitors; flies were everywhere. The town is a large oasis with hundreds of thousands of palm trees. One Palmeraie just outside the town claims to have more than two hundred thousand date palms, along with figs and pomegranates. I wonder how many flies?

In olden times, before the advent of motor vehicles, Tozeur was an important transit depot for transportation by camel train through the Sahara and beyond. Founded by the Romans, the town was named Tusuros, growing to become an important Roman outpost. Later, it flourished as a trading and transit point for the slave trade. Many locals claim to be descended from those slaves.

Leaving Tozeur was not easy, the time spent there was just too 'happy and comfortable'. Though it was good to be 'fly-free'.

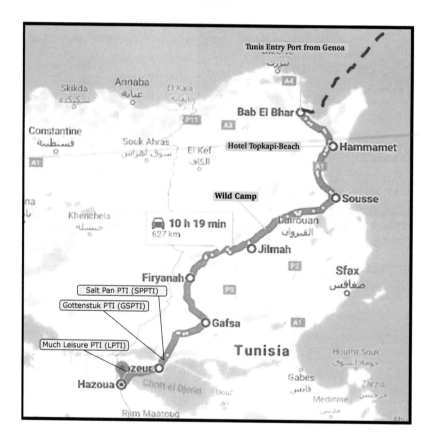

Chapter 15
Algerian Frontier PTI

Thinking we knew all there was to know about border control, we learnt a whole new chapter on entering Algeria.

Leaving the customs post from Tunisia was smooth, efficient and friendly. No way could we have foreseen the experience about to confront us as we entered Algeria. Progress was seriously **PTI**ed at the Hazoua Frontier Oasis. The border post into Algeria is just a short distance south west of the friendly Tunisian town of Tozeur.

First our mandatory escort, for militarily controlled Algeria, was well over an hour late arriving to meet us. Then the task of getting Boudie and Tasca through customs was beyond anything I have ever experienced in Africa, or elsewhere during a lifetime of worldwide travel. It was a new, exhausting, though educational experience for all of us.

The Customs Officers, though well mannered, were more than meticulous with the inspection of our vehicles and contents. They were well beyond being long winded with their decision making and administrative processing. Appearing keen to be on our way made them even more finickity, so we tried to relax, leaving them to their pedantic ways. Maybe they were just grateful for something to do in this lonely spot in the desert! 'Overenthusiastic' would be an inadequate portrayal of their endeavours. Each ammo box, storage drawer and bag were opened, unpacked and meticulously searched through. Our overloaded Landys attracted them like a swarm of bees to nectar laden flowers in full bloom. Customs officials were 'everywhere'. If they could find the slightest reason to remove items from the vehicles, they did so. I should have heeded Robert Jefferson's advice from 1907 re 'overloading'.

The advice to 'Take just a box of tools' was lodged in my head!

Every detail of each vehicle was examined and recorded. This and all the paperwork were carried out manually and very tediously; moving from desk to desk at a snail's pace. Where were the computers? Not one to be seen anywhere. Boudie attracted much more attention from the 'worker bees' than Tasca did. Maybe it was her 'military' shape, or her yellow 'honey' colour finish seducing the 'honeybees' to hover over her looking for yet more nectar. We were after all in a military controlled country. I'm so pleased I resprayed her in a 'non-military' colour before leaving the UK.

The confiscated items included our binoculars and the all-important two-way radios. They simply cut the wires and took the radio sets from the vehicles, leaving us with just the handsets, aerials and the severed protruding wires. Fortunately, our cameras, phones and Lap Tops aroused no interest for them.

Arriving at the border at around three in the afternoon; it was gone ten that night when we departed with the paperwork and receipts for all the confiscated items. This was indeed a long lesson in 'Border Control Meddling & Confiscation' (BCM&CPTI).

Our plans did not include returning through Hazoua; we intended driving south through Algeria then into Niger and beyond; little did we know!

The Trophy almost couldn't hack it here, though we all muddled through – like the CTM we were 'upside down' by now!!!

At long last we were on our way south into Algeria, the source of more Landylife 'experience' tales.

Chapter 16
Sandy Desert

Not unexpectedly the occasional **PTI** befell us in the desert, which of course, were mostly self-imposed and enjoyable. Losing traction in the desert sand, during the hot mid-day sun, is far from difficult, especially with All Terrain 'knobbly' tyres that love to dig into the soft sand. Here we are when Tasca stubbornly refused to move either forward or backward. Rather than let her sink up to her axles Boudie's winch was again put to good use making a simple recovery, being sure to maintain momentum once she was rolling again.

Desert sand is firm to drive on in the cool of the morning or late evening. However, it becomes soft, offering little by way of firmness or density during the midday heat. Smooth treaded

*This was **B**rew **PTI (BPTI)** brought on by Fixer's desire for a brew; not that any of us had any objection to that. OK we paid the price, but it was fun and all part of our 'Landy Experience'.*

tyres and low pressures are best. The AT tyres we had fitted helped us, once again, find that place called 'Gottenstuk', which is great fun when you get there, so why complain when you arrive at a pleasurable **G**ottenstuk **S**andy **PTI (GSPTI).**

We had to remind ourselves that the fun of driving in the sand, though great, was not the reason for of our being in the desert. We were on our way through Algeria, Niger, Nigeria and Cameroon then via the Congo to Malawi and on to South Africa. We continued to enjoy the stunning Saharan Desert, the happenings, the remoteness, the eeriness and calmness along with the enjoyable challenges we met along the way. Night time walks were particularly enchanting, looking up at the stars in the crystal-clear skies and following the camel spoor. From these footprints you envisage there being hundreds of camels wandering around, though you rarely spot one wandering in the wild openness. The silence in the night-time desert resonates loud in your ears.

A memorable Land Rover 'experience' was reaped as every kilometre passed, despite the compulsory ever present but pleasant 'guide' and the Police/Military presence. Security must provide the highest level of employment in Algeria, since there are reputedly some twenty-two eyes covertly watching you at any time? Despite the constant hassle created they were after all, just doing the job they were paid to do. Most were civil-ish in going about their duties. When handled in a polite and calm manner, they could be understanding and helpful.

From the border we drove some 1,200km to the town of Ain Salah. Along the way we were prevented, by the constant security presence, from visiting a lot of the many interesting sights. Like their owners, Land Rovers enjoy, and indeed crave, a rest now and again, all classed as **PTI**. These **S**ocial **PTI**s **(SPTI)** were those moments which leisure made even more enjoyable when joining with the locals to play 'Desert Dominoes' or enjoy

'Creative' music played on ingenious homemade instruments. We drank surprisingly good clear, cold water from goat skins hanging in trees or at roadside stalls.

We spent some Magical moments amongst nomadic Tuareg families living in the desert where they tend their camels and goats. They were so welcoming, happy, and a pleasure to be amongst. They see no troubles in the world and certainly have no desire to cause any.

'**B**aking' **PTI**s **(BPTI)** featured several times when kneaded Semolina dough is put onto hot ashes in a pre-prepared hole in

Desert music   *Desert dominoes*

Happy Tuaregs living in the desert

the sand. The dough is then covered with sand and left to bake. When baked the loaf is taken from the ashes, the sand cleaned off. The baked bread is then broken up and layered with slices of roast lamb, veggies and the sauce the lamb was cooked in. The outcome always was yet another unforgettable and agreeable **E**ating **PTI. (EPTI).**

Tea was taken often, usually 'mint' tea, either made in the desert on an open fire, or relished at a roadside cafe'. Desert tea is made using two pots; water is boiled on a fire in a fire blackened pot, mint leaves are put into a clean pot, the boiling water is then poured over them. It is left for a while then poured seven times back and forth from pot to pot.

Much sugar is added then it's served up in small glasses to drink creating a pleasing **Tea TPI (TTPI).**

Land Rover **PTI**s in the desert are 100% enjoyable.

Thank you, Land Rover, for bringing us **'By Far so Far'**.

Chapter 17
Saharan & Desert Surprises

Sahara gateway

We continued on our sandy way downwards, through Algeria, north to south, across the Sahara Desert in the direction of Niger towards the I-n-Guezzam/Assakka border post, some 2,500km away. The border is about 375km south of the nearest town, Tamanrasset. As we left Tunisia at Hazoua we were warned that camping was not permitted anywhere between the border and the next Algerian town. Having entered Algeria late at night, tired and frustrated by the lengthy border **PTI**, we opted to avoid security hassle by staying at a recommended hotel in El Oued.

Known as the city of a thousand domes, it was built over many years to provide homes and shelter from the fierce Saharan sun. The city is sited over an underground river which supplies more than adequate water supplies all the year round. This water enables brick production, making El Oued one of the very few brick-built towns in a desert.

Again, the locals were polite and friendly, even though security was very evident and active. A plain clothed security guard appeared beside me warning me that photographing in public was an offence as I took a picture of the national flag painted on a wall. I managed to convince him I had deleted the image. I fear that was a little white lie. This was nearly a **PTI** by **D**etention (**DPTI)**

Later the same guy popped up out of nowhere when I went to Boudie in the Hotel car park; "just checking" he said. Next morning, he again materialised beside me as I walked along the street. I had just visited three banks, each of which was unable to change either the US Dollars or UK Pounds that I had with me into the local Dinar. He kindly guided me to a bank that did change money, which was more difficult than I ever expected. When I came out of the bank, after a lengthy friendly chat with the manager, there he was, waiting for me. This time he was in his bakkie ready to take me back to the hotel, or wherever I wished to go. Later that day, with a few friends, he took us around town to local visitor attractions, though we were not sure if he was 'on the make', it was however a pleasant experience.

Time to 'hit the road' once more. Ahead the route, known as the 'Route du Hoggar', passes through amazing mountain terrain, from Tunis to Agadez, some 3,800km. Things went well as we pressed on in the general direction of Tamanrasset where we would collect our entry visas for entry into Niger. They were all made ready before we left the UK, at least that's as I was led to believe by the Niger embassy in London. I had submitted the forms, spoken several times by phone with the immigration officer who assured me the Visas would awaiting collection at the border for us. "Just visit the Niger ambassador in Tamanrasset, he will fix you up" were his exact words to me; made in good faith I'm sure. Perhaps I should have been a little more wary, as my passport went missing for two weeks in the Algerian Embassy in London during the application process.

Once into Niger I was planning to visit the city of Agadez, the world's largest 'mud city'. The buildings are primarily of cob construction, made of mostly, as expected, mud. One such building, a minaret, at 127 feet tall, is the tallest cob construction in the world. Agadez is inhabited by Tuaregs, a people we came to find very agreeable when we met them in the desert. Agadez is known as 'The True Gateway to The Desert'.

On our southerly way we came upon the interesting town of Touggourt. It was from here in 1922 that five Citroen half-tracks set off to traverse the Sahara into Niger.

They were successful and claimed the first Saharan vehicular crossing. I'm not sure why all the fuss Mr. Citroen, a Land Rover can do that very easily on just four wheels!

Citroen half-tracks

Outside Touggourt we were taken to visit a derelict Grand Estate house with a huge Palmieri on land we were told once belonged to Mr. Citroen. I've not found any proof of the Citroen connection other than the word of the guide who showed us around; after all he was a church minister! Was this a **S**acred **C**itroen **(SCPTI)**?

I repent Land Rover for this fleeting Citroen 'infidelity'.

Driving south the roads were good, well, where there were any. It was now time to enter the Sahara Desert proper. Rounding a bend, we spotted something that looked like military activity on the tops of headlands both sides of us. Before fully grasping the situation, we were surrounded by the armed military from atop those bluffs. At first, we feared the worst. This 'terrorising' **PTI** slowly turned into more friendly banter; once they were assured that we brought no ill intent with us. I'm sure they were pleased we came along to ignite some real live action for them to engage with.

They may have had a long wait for the next passing vehicle to scare the living 'sh-1-t' out of with their **SH*1*T PTI (SH1TPTI)**

From then on driving through the desert was free of the persistent and irritable security checks, such as we had to contend with on the highways. For now, there were no 'secret eyes' watching our every move; or at least that's how we felt. Although the checks were a nuisance, with a few exceptions, they were handled in a reasonably polite and amiable manner.

Each time our papers and passports were scrutinised, approved, signed off and stamped, allowing us to be on our way to the next check point. The whole rigmarole took anything from five minutes to an hour or more to complete. Most often this occurred when driving into a town, then again on the way out. When in or near built-up areas we had to identify the campsite or hostelry we intended to spend the coming night. If not, they would designate an overnight location to us. If it was approaching dark, after which time we were forbidden to drive, they escorted us to a campsite, Hotel, Auberge, or wherever they chose. At most control points the personnel we came across were, mostly, friendly and helpful. Some sites we were sent to at times were somewhat dubious and a couple extremely so, causing 'Irritability' **PTIs. (IPTI)**

Maybe an understatement, but there is an abundance of sand in the Sahara Desert! Beautiful to behold, amazing to drive through, it is also superb for wild camping. Bear in mind, there aren't any Filling Stations, bars, restaurants, cafes or Hotels to be found in the desert; but then isn't that a very good reason for being there? We enjoyed plenty of sand driving without being irresponsible.

In the middle of nowhere we came across a post with a sign, with two large bullet holes in, pointing out the route of the long cancelled, because of terrorist threats, 2011 London to Cape Town Car Rally. These indicator posts would have been about the only way to make progress through the wide-open desert.

This was a superb Land Rover 'Experience' territory for us to delight in many **S**andy & **G**ottenstuk **PTI (S&GPTI)**

Boudie at Desert Sandy Gottenstuk

Mohamed took us to an amazing oasis amidst the desolation of the Sahara. Where does all that water come from? We spent time at the oasis, with our gentle, friendly and knowledgeable guide. It was our pleasure having have Mohamed onboard with us.

*A **P**leasant **O**asis **PTI (POPTI)***

Progress was later slowed by the Hoggar Mountains with its wall of 'Rock Army'. An eerie sight, a wonder to behold, hence the name 'Route du Hoggard', some 1,000 meters above sea level, peaking at 2,000 meters and covering over two hundred square miles. Tasca looked miniscule at the foot of the unmoving stone warriors. The Hoggar Mountains make Ideal Land Rover terrain.

Rock Army with Tasca dwarfed at the base

It was here, amongst those rugged, ragged, rocks that Boudie suffered her first, and only, **P**uncture **PTI. (PPTI)** of this trip.

After a four-hour drive along the jagged tracks up the mountain towards the peak we came upon the Hamlet of Assekreem. Here we spent a comfortable night with a few Tuareg locals looking after us. We were well fed, entertained and made to feel very comfortable and at home. The next morning, after climbing a few hundred steps I came upon a lone building of no architectural interest. I found it to be an 'Hermitage' built in 1911 by a once wealthy German, Charles Foucauld. He left his fortune behind in Germany to live in this mountainous region and dwell amongst the local Tuareg people to share their lives and hardships.

The stones, and other building materials, used in the construction of the hermitage were easily found very close to hand. Everything else had to be carried by man and camel from many kilometres away and up the steep mountain side. To this day all requisites, such as water, food and other domestic needs are carted in this same way. By way of compensation the views are stunning. Assekrem translates to the 'End of the World'

Sunset at Assekrem

which is where you feel you are when looking out over the flabbergasting panorama. I fully understand Charles Foucauld's affection for the region.

Foucauld converted to Catholicism and founded the order of the 'Little Brothers of Jesus'. A religious order accepted and protected by the Islamic Algerian government, then and today. From 1912 to 1916 he cared for the locals in both spiritual and humanitarian ways. Sadly, he was murdered by robbers in 1916 whilst he was away from the Hermitage. Since then there has been a continual succession of Brothers of Jesus at the Hermitage. We were welcomed and shown around by the most charming, gentle current resident, Brother Edward.

Charles Foucauld's interesting original writings are there to be seen amongst many other fascinating Artefacts from past and present. A calm **Hermitage PTI (HPTI)** Halt.

Nearby we encountered our first challenge to Land Rover's claim of being **'The Best 4x4 by Far'**. A cameleer driving his camel train 'off-road' claimed he could go 'further by far' on a camel than we could in a Land Rover. A challenge we did not take up at the time as we needed our Landys to go a 'lot further by far' yet. None the less we saw it as an interesting challenge to be considered in the future. Indeed, a challenge we were to take up later. This was a **PTI** in waiting?

Later, Mohamed met a friend of his in this sparse vast open desert. No idea how he got there, where he came from or indeed where he was going. They chatted for at least an hour. Chatting over, the friend simply vanished; just where did he go after this **'Verbal' PTI. (VPTI).**

Venturing onward across the mostly harsh and empty landscape we continued south toward our next target, the Algerian border with Niger. The occasional **Map Reading PTI (MRPTI)** was a must, though not necessary as we were driving across desert in a sort of SSW direction There weren't any roads at all and

Mohamed meets an old friend in the desert

certainly very few landmarks, apart from a ruined French Fort and water troughs we stumbled across very occasionally.

Map Reading was just another excuse for a rest and a brew. The map didn't tell us much, other than confirm we were in a desert. Ethel, our very basic GPS, showed a straight line most of the time, pointing us in a 'general direction' south. More recent versions of GPS are rather more sophisticated and 'knowledgeable'.

Thank you, Land Rover you have once more took us 'Above and Beyond'.

Chapter 18

Niger Border

Our tour through Algeria brought us eventually to the busy southern city of Tamanrasset. Entry of course, was preceded by the now routine visit to the Police Station to register our arrival in town. We pitched camp that first night at a good site on the edge of town.

Tamanrasset, where temperatures often exceed 47°C, is known as the 'Heart of the Sahara'. The city was established many years ago, as a military outpost to protect the trans-Saharan trade routes. Tamanrasset is an oasis where, despite the difficult climate, citrus fruits, apricots, dates, almonds, cereals and figs are all grown a plenty. Nomadic Tuareg people are the town's main inhabitants, indeed it is their major Algerian city. When we got there the dates were ripe; as in Tozeur the flies were everywhere!

Having enjoyed a good overnight's camp, it was time to visit the border control office to collect our 'pre-arranged' visas for the next leg of our journey into Niger. Purposely we got there early, to find the queue was already very long and chaos reigned. After a while staff came out, put up the shutters, and with much flapping of arms and yelling they managed to break up the by now manic crowd. Turning to our friendly guide Mohamed for an explanation; he too was confused. Eventually we were told "No visas or border crossing today. All are closed". Unable to find any reason why, Mohamed tried his best to glean some information from the staff, without result.

After waiting for what seemed for ever, we discovered the border into Niger was closed. This was thanks to Al-Qaeda, who prior to our arrival, kidnapped five French engineers; hence the border closure. This surely was an **Al-Qaeda PTI (AQPTI).**

Mohamed then evaporated, simply melting away into the ether, never to be seen again. By law we are always to be accompanied by a full-time approved guide; we were now falling foul of that law. Almost as expected, 'Landy-Luck' materialised to find us the most idyllic accommodation just out of the town. It was the best place to stay with the most wonderful hostess, assistant and guide, all in one amazing lady, Claudia. Together with her adopted son, Younus, she made us most welcome and proved to be of great help.

We stayed at her Auberge, 'Gite Saharien', hoping soon to make the crossing into Niger. In fact, this turned out to be the most comfortable and pleasant **G**ite **S**aharien **(GSPTI).**

We really wanted to continue our trek via Niger, Nigeria, Cameroon and on through the Congo, for some Land Rover mud fun. On the way we hoped to visit Malawi as we were raising funds for an orphanage in Lilongwe.

Fortunately, Claudia we soon realised, carried considerable influence in and around Tamanrasset, also her husband was involved in local affairs. Unfortunately, at the time of our visit he was stuck in Niger, as a result of the border closure. He was tending a herd of camels he farmed in Niger at the time.

Claudia accompanied us to the Niger deputy ambassador's office at the control post. Managing to get a 'foot in the door' she introduced us to the local ambassador. I found him to be the most helpful polite, professional and proficient person you could wish to meet. He sincerely wanted to help, but as he understood it at the time, there was no possibility of crossing the border for at least the next six days. He put me in touch with the Chief of Police in northern Niger who I spoke with several times over the phone.

He too was yet another most understanding, willing and helpful man. The situation was now becoming very clear. He explained that under normal circumstances we would have to join a military convoy to be escorted as far as Agadez in the centre of Niger. That would have been fine, and indeed as we expected. As all the Police and Military personnel were now busy hunting down the terrorists and those poor French hostages there was no way he could put a convoy together. "Keep in touch" he said, which we did. We stayed on for a while at Claudia's and let events take their turn. We took the opportunity to enjoy the local markets, cafes and restaurants brought about by this **N**iger **B**order **PTI (NBPTI)**

Tasca seized the opportunity to call into a local garage to have her oils changed and have some minor welding done on a suffering rear shock absorber bracket. This **S**hock **A**bsorber **PTI (SAPTI)** was soon fixed.

A day or so after settling in we were ordered by the local Police to cease driving around town unescorted in our English registered vehicles. So, we took to the surrounding desert area for some 'off-roading'.

The imposing Anderson Mountains were behind Claudia's Auberge. We did try, but no we weren't able get to the very top in the Landys, we felt it wise not to call upon Landy-Luck at this time! Returning to Claudia's, we were once again cautioned about driving our vehicles unescorted.

Clever Claudia introduced us to some local cameleers who she felt could satisfy our 'off-roading' desires and perhaps keep us out of trouble. The intention being to hide us from the prying eyes of the authorities and avoid further brushes with the law for the few days whilst waiting for the border to re-open. Recalling the earlier Camel versus Land Rover challenge, we agreed to go into the desert aboard camels to test this alternative off-roader. This would be rather like a road test, so we made appraisals; as they do in the motoring world.

Demo' models brought to us for selection

Very soon a few camels were brought along for us to select our preferred, and with the cameleer's advice, pick a suitable steed. They seemed somewhat daunting at first, but very soon revealed great friendliness, willingness and enthusiasm to take us anywhere 'off-road'. Any doubts we may have harboured soon dissolved as these 'off-roaders' set out to prove their worth. My camel soon became a friend to be trusted.

By day he was a good '4x4er', by night he ambled off to get up to whatever camels do at night. Without fail he was back ready willing and able early in the morning for another full day; but oh boy, did his breath stink!

Your breath stinks

After a few days of 'test driving' it was a difficult task to decide which is the best 4x4. I do appreciate the Camel's many varied skills and capabilities; also, camel overall running and maintenance costs do appear to be extremely low.

I awarded the camels many 'Camel Trophies' and appreciated their many diverse abilities and capabilities.

84

In conclusion, camels may be suited for many tasks, but they do fall behind the Land Rover in the areas of accessibility to the driver's seat, comfort, speed and control. Camels do tend to have a mind of their own, not that Land Rovers don't, but camels do tend to go their own way at times! I say all this having not passed a Camel Driving Test!

One camel plus being that when all else fails at the end of the day camel meat is delicious! *(Apologies to vegetarians and vegans)*. It makes for easy environmentally friendly recycling when compared to writing off end of life vehicles.

Camels do exhaust drivers

I was told a Cameleers diet consists of seven dates a day, edible ones that is, along with a sip of olive oil and camel milk, all readily available to hand. I haven't tried it, though I do like olives, olive oil and dates.

Overall though Land Rover does live up to its claim of being:

'THE BEST 4X4 BY FAR'

You can take a Landy to more places more comfortably and Land Rovers, with care live longer than camels.

In conclusion, whilst camels may be well suited to certain specific areas and tasks, they do fall behind Land Rover in respect of comfort, protection from the elements and control. I'm not so sure about the levels of fun and capability in all terrains and winching though.

A great way to spend a **C**amel **R**oad **T**est **PTI (CRTPTI).**

Test results on next page:

	Camel	Land Rover LWT
Yr. manufactured	Circa 10,000BC to date.	1971-1985
Dimensions:- *Track:* *Width:* *Length:* *Weight:*	*1m* *0.75m* *2m* *600kg*	*1.33m* *1.68m* *3.62m* *1,318kg*
Angles of:- *Approach:* *Departure:* *Clearance:*	*90deg* *90deg* *2.5m*	*49deg* *32deg* *203mm*
Engine:	*Large Single Heart, 2 Lungs & many Arteries, Veins and Muscles.*	*2.25l 4cyl petrol OHV - 2286cc 3 bearing crank*
Fuel System:	*Big Heart pump.*	*Solex or Zenith*
Gearbox:	*Fully automatic forward, reverse and sideways gears.*	*4 forward gears. Reverse gear and overdrive.*
Emissions:	*Large turds, so dry they can be used as 'firewood' or 'building blocks' immediately. Methane gas.*	*Lead/Carbon*
K/L:	*16km/L Water, released from the hump*	*Petrol 9km/L*
Max speed:	*65km/hr*	*100km/hr*
Range/tank	*3,000km*	*810km*
Fuel Tank capacity:	*200L (one tank)*	*90L (Two tanks)*
Tyres:	*4x4 soft 'wing toed' extreme off-road pads. Puncture proof.*	*Michelin MX*
Suspension:	*Fully flexible Knees, ankles and hips with auto terrain response. Lowers for access and loading.*	*Coils springs + 2" lift – fixed*
Hill descent:	*Built in - fully automatic.*	*No.*
Brakes:	*Instant acting, muscle controlled with built-in collision avoidance.*	*Drums – front and rear*

Chapter 19
Leaving Tamanrasset

After that enjoyable 'Camel Experience' it was back to the border once again, only to find it still firmly closed; and likely to remain so for at least the foreseeable future. In fact, it remains closed to this very day.

I cannot praise enough the remarkable attempts by Claudia, the Niger Ambassador and the Northern Niger Chief of Police, for all their helpful and well-meaning efforts. We are especially grateful for the lengthy endeavours Claudia and Younus went to on our behalf.

We considered and costed several alternative plans to unimpede our progress. Do we fly with the Landys from Tamanrasset to Agadez? After weighting up the cost of hiring a plane and other expenses, the amounts just didn't fit our budget. An alternative would have been to truck the Landys to Agadez, Zinder or Niamey while we fly from Algeria to meet them. None of these ideas were doable as we still had to get them across the closed border. I wonder, would our Landys still be at the border today had we left them there.

Other options considered included driving back all the way through Algeria to the Mediterranean coast to ship them from the port of Oran to Nigeria, Cameroon or the Congo. Or ship them from Oran to Eritrea on the east coast to continue, the more normal route, on through Ethiopia, Kenya, Tanzania, and Malawi then on Southwards.

We stopped over for a couple more days in Tamanrasset; well at least until we were ordered to 'get out of Algeria', as they were concerned about more possible terrorist activities.

Our papers, on demand, were presented at the Gendarmerie in the afternoon to have them prepared, signed off and ready for departure early the next morning.

We were then to be escorted out of the country by the security forces employing their 'Hasslement' **PTI (HPTI)** methods. *(Hasslement being a new word I created to fit the circumstance)*

That last evening, we spent with Claudia and Younus over an enjoyable dinner. It was going to be tough leaving such a tranquil spot and to bid farewell to the unique Claudia who had been of such help and comfort to us.

As dictated by security, it was to be an early departure; 6:30am when we were to meet our newly appointed guide, Abdullah, for the hand over process. Not unexpectedly, what should have taken no more than ten minutes, took another hour and a half to repeat the process we had already completed the previous afternoon. We did our best to remain calm, it drove us to become very irritated and frustrated. Have you ever had that feeling of having overstayed your welcome, by an **I**rritation and **F**rustration **PTI? (I&FPTI).**

Before leaving, Claudia warned us not to discuss matters with our new guide, with the words "the devil wears many faces", inferring that he could be an informant. Paps very soon renamed him Goofy. Bidding farewell to Claudia and Younus was not easy.

Off we went under Goofy's escort; he rode in Tasca with Fixer. We sped off from Tamanrasset to a time schedule based upon the speed of the escort's more modern vehicle rather than Boudie's somewhat more limited ability. This led to late night arrivals at most of the pre-arranged overnight halts and a very exhausted, though happy Boudie. The route involved many more 'security' checks; most taking the normal 30 to 45 minutes, generating even more irritation. Why don't the Algerian Security service and the Intelligence Services have a computer network, or at least recognise their own security personnel?

On the way we passed through In Salah once more. Entering town there was of course the anticipated security check on the outskirts, aggravated when in the centre of town, we were taken to the Police Station for a further two hour 'clearance'; this at nine thirty at night. By now after a long day we were hot, fed up, tired and beyond hunger. Anger was also vented toward the Swiss Agent who endorsed our venture into Algeria; they were aware the country was virtually closed for some months prior to our actual arrival. Had we known from the outset we would have selected an alternative route.

This really was a **PTI** by **S**wiss **A**gent **(SAPTI).**

Paps chatted up a policeman who found us a campsite very akin to a waste tip, which was not an option. After further 'negotiation' the policeman found us a hotel the 'Hotel de Ville'; not much better, thought it did have beds, of sorts. We crashed out until our departure early the next morning.

Of course, our leaving was met with yet another 'clearance' on exiting the town. I was annoyed at having to make the back-tracks, although I did sort of understand the reasons behind it. It was a lot of hassle, but as ever we made it as enjoyable as we could, it was the only way to remain sane.

The people we encountered along the way were again, almost without exception, helpful and friendly. Most were after all, just doing what they were paid to do.

As we drove into our next town we were greeted by Ahmed, a friend of Claudia's who we were very comfortable with.

He took us back to his impressive one hundred and thirty-year-old Auberge, where we were royally entertained. There being no Wi-Fi available, Ahmed took Paps and I to a local cybercafe, once we found one that was not chock-a-block with enthusiastic 'cyberiets'. It took us some five hours to get done; the greatest hurdle being that most of the keyboards were in Arabic; no QUERTYS around! A real **K**ey **B**oard **PTI (KBPTI).**

Meanwhile, while we were 'cybering', Fixer took the time to check over Boudie and Tasca. At the Same time Ahmed set about filling the swimming pool for us to take a dip, despite there being a serious drought at the time; Fixer's efforts to stop him failed.

That evening we spent with Ahmed, he in his Berber dress suit, at a Mosabite music festival. An amazing evening with of course no alcohol! Morality Guards were in attendance to ensure all males and females in the audience kept apart; males to the left, females to the right. They all had fun. The guards ignored a couple from a French film crew filming the event, who were having a great time dancing away together in the isle. This was a very enjoyable **R**esting **PTI (RPTI).**

Next morning, we really missed our two-way radios as Fixer, with 'Goofy' on board Tasca, bolted off up a long steep hill out of town. With no means of communication, we felt lost as we climbed up the hill with all the speed Boudie could muster, not knowing where they had gone. We found Tasca some way off along the road. The frustrations, and Goofy were proving too much for Fixer, he just had to 'let off steam'.

I must say we were feeling much about the same, we were all perhaps over 'Goofied'.

A delicious 'poulet' lunch stop refreshed us. It was now that we realised that "Goofy" was not a real guide and was unable to speak a word of English and had no idea which way to direct us. Claudia's words were ringing in my ears as 'Goofy', somehow convinced us he knew the direct route to the border, as he said he had spoken personally to all the police and gendarmerie en route.

Claiming to be a policeman 'Goofy' then jumped into another car with two male occupants and rudely gesticulated us to follow them. Paps suggested that perhaps they were not policeman at all. Our suspicions were aroused so we pulled them over and asked to see their police IDs. None of them were police or indeed any form of security officials, proving to be a real **F**ake **P**olice **PTI (FPPTI).**

Thank you once more Claudia for your wise words as we left you at Tamanrasset. From then we went on unescorted towards the border with Tunisia with Landy-Luck at our side.

Tunisia to Niger 'and back' Fun and Disappointments

Tunisia to Niger 'and back' Fun and Disappointments

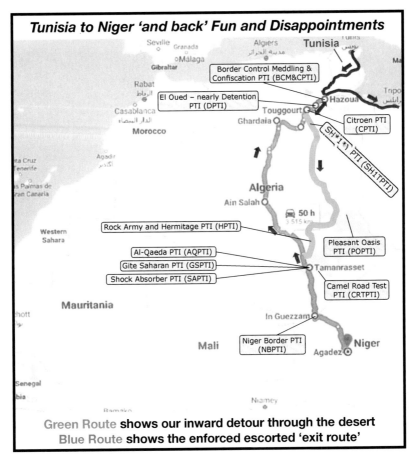

Green Route **shows our inward detour through the desert**
Blue Route **shows the enforced escorted 'exit route'**

Chapter 20
Algeria/Tunisia border

Thanks to Al-Qaeda, we are now, several weeks later, reluctantly back at the Hazoua Frontier Oasis border post on our way back into Tunisia. Drawing up at the control point we fully expected problems after our last 'Confiscating Experience' here. Was this to be yet another chapter of our now extended 'African Border Control Apprenticeship'? Not at all, it was like a meeting of long-lost friends. They recognised and welcomed us, reminding us of the collection of items they had those weeks before confiscated, which they would now happily return. All we had to do was show them the receipts they had given us on entering the country. Paps and Fixer instantly handed over their receipts, but as is not unusual, I couldn't find mine, and yes, the bulk of the 'bits' were taken from me. Without hesitation they produced a copy of the receipt for me in minutes. After a short while back came the two-way radios, binoculars and all the other confiscated paraphernalia without a quibble.

We spent a long while engaged in friendly tete-a-tete and banter at their office. I just could not believe these characters were the same ones who confronted us those weeks before on our way into Algeria. They were interested in our tales of travel and experiences in their country. They genuinely shared with us our disappointment over the events and the reason we were back at their border control.

It was now late in the evening. The senior officer announced he was now off duty and asked us to wait while he changed into his civvies and gather for coffee, butty and chat. He soon returned in traditional robes and off we went to the canteen whiling away time over several coffees, snacks and much banter.

An unexpected bonus was the return of our confiscated gear and the freedom from the 'spying eyes'. As we parted, they guided us to a safe 'wild' campsite not far from the border, which as promised, turned out to be a quiet and comfortable spot.

This was an unexpected happy end to the rush back through Algeria. We were anxious to get moving. Our time spent in Algeria, while not as expected, or as planned, was all the same a fascinating and pleasurable experience even though 'hassled', especially by the unfortunate return to Tunisia.

I award them a Camel Trophy for their friendliness upon our return, a complete **U-TURN PTI (UTPTI).**

Landy-Luck was with us all the way. To be leaving Algeria in one piece was 'a pleasure' and another 'experience'.

Returned **C**onfiscated **G**oods **PTI (RCGPTI)**.

Thank you also Landy-Luck.

Onward to the Tunisia border post.

Chapter 21
Back into Tunisia

We were psyched up over a challenge facing us crossing into Tunisia; Pap's Visa was for a single entry into Tunisia, she was not covered for this unexpected return visit. The Visa had to be revised and signed off by the local Consulate to validate it, before re-entering into Tunisia. It's late in the evening, where do we find an ambassador? Thankfully the affable officials at the customs post managed to locate him. He was taking dinner somewhere in Tunis; too far for us to go at that time of day. I don't know how, but they managed to speak to him. The Visa was 'miraculously' signed off by, I'm not sure who! The fee was 10 whatever notes we had 10 of to pay with. Surely Landy-Luck was on our side once more! It was almost eleven thirty at night when we eventually left the Tunisian entry border.

A couple of kilometres along the road we turned off down a side track where we pulled up, pitched our tents and crashed out for the night. It proved to be a quiet, comfortable and restful spot. We were in desperate need of rest, so probably wouldn't have noticed anything. We were awoken early, in the pre-dawn light, by scratching sounds only to find some jackals busy around the tent. In the morning light we could see our 'cosy' spot had been occupied by many a traveller before us. The jackals were just clearing up the detritus left by thoughtless campers adding to the world's litter problems. The Jackals were acting as unpaid environmental recyclers.

Fixer decided it was time for him to return home to the UK, feeling he had now been away from his building business far too long. After all, he had expected to have reached South Africa, dropped off Tasca, and flown home in less time. It was difficult saying good bye as he was part of our team, we had good times; despite those sporadic frustrations outside our control. He was an invaluable team member as he could fix or improvise most things Landy. Pointing him in the right direction for home off he went in Tasca. Happily, he and Tasca experienced a **PTI** free drive back home.

Boudie, Paps and I carried on our adventure through Southern Tunisia wondering what would be next. Me being the 'stubborn old 'Gruffalo' that I am, was determined to get Boudie to my home in the Western Cape whatever. The first option was to change plans and drive, the much used, easier route down the eastern side of the African continent. The 'easy route', so I thought, was to follow on through Tunisia, Libya, Egypt, North and South Sudan, Ethiopia, Kenya, Tanzania, Malawi, Zimbabwe, Zambia, Botswana then south through South Africa to the Western Cape. Simply follow the old, much travelled, Cairo to Cape road believing it would be **PTI** free all the way home.

Our next border crossing would be from Tunisia into Libya, a visa could be acquired at the border. This was just before Western interference and the Gaddafi war, followed by the sad and on-going turmoil in that country. Rather than going directly to the border we explored southern Tunisia, most of which we found to be beautiful, colourful and tranquil. Apart that is from some tourist attractions such as the run-down film sets from some of yet more Star Wars scenes. The locals were so friendly, pleasant, helpful, sharing and joyful to be amongst.

While driving around I fancied a spot of house hunting. One empty home I found was 'unique'; located in an idyllic, tranquil rural location, high in the hills with glorious views of the surrounding remoteness. The interior was spacious and very cool, certainly unique! Unfortunately, it required rather too much renovation to bring it up to scratch in the time I had available. Sadly, I had to give it a miss. This **House Hunting PTI (HHPTI)** would have been a hit on the BBC's Escape to the Country programme.

'Unique' house hunting opportunity

Here we are, in our heavily overloaded Boudie, negotiating a wide range of road surfaces, feeling a **PTI** could not be far away. Sure enough, as if planned, a clanking noise joined us from the rear left quarter. Oh dear, a shock absorber had broken off its bracket bringing on a case of **S**hock **A**bsorbing **PTI (SAPTI).** When you are in a spot of bother Landy-Luck is always close by I reminded myself. True to form, Landy-Luck quickly came to our aide when around fifteen minutes later, down the road we happened upon a welder working away in his roadside workshop. This good man soon had us welded up, unimpeded and on our way.

Before setting out on our expedition I had changed Boudie's

comfy parabolic springs for heavy duty springs. This was necessary as Boudie was resting on her bump-stops when loaded up with all the gear, which we thought at the time, was essential. Those same springs I later had modified.

On our way we encountered much heavy traffic as we meandered around, such as the occasional donkey and cart or scooter. Oh, what a wonderful pace of life! Of course, we did visit tourist spots as well, though preferring to keep clear of them.

The salt pans we unexpectadly came across, in fact the main bulk of the pan Chott el Jerrid, where we had 'gottenstuk' on our way out were stunning sights. It was fascinating to watch folk harvesting the salt.

Even more amazing were the beautiful rock roses that 'grow' in those pans. This brought about a '**S**alty' **PTI (SPTI).** At the pans we met a couple who invited us to dine at their home; that night we slept out on their flat roof; what stunning views.

Rock Roses

We refuelled at one of the many, 'Can and Funnel' re-fuelling 'stations', near the border. Both Libyans and Tunisians were driving their bakkies illegally back and forth across the border in remote areas loaded with barrels and cans of cheap and plentiful Libyan petrol and diesel. This **L**ibyan **F**uel **PTI (LFPTI)** provided the cheapest fuel I had ever found, and it wasn't diluted with water, as experienced in some other remote areas in the past.

Can & Funnel Filling Station

Nearby, we came upon the **B**est **V**alue **L**ibyan **C**ash **PTI (BVLCPTI)** who obliged us with a very good deal. This 'Exchange Bureau' consisted of an elderly gentleman, sitting on a plastic chair in the shade, waving a hand full of notes for all to see.

The officials at this border were the most helpful and friendly people you could meet. They were interested to hear of our recent experiences and appreciated our situation. However, they

Friendly Exchange Bureau

held firm that we could not enter Libya without an entry visa. They wouldn't even let us enter and rest up in the 'no-mans' land, as they were sure we would be refused entry in to Libya. Most likely we would be sent back, and they would be unable to allow us re-entry into Tunisia, as our existing visas were single entry. The issues surrounding the issue of new Tunisian visas would create a problematic **Libyan Entry Visa PTI (LEVPTI).**

Some hard thinking was called for, so we headed back into Ben Gardane, found and booked into a newly renovated hotel, which was a delight. Everyone there was very friendly and helpful. The young man at reception even took us into town to a recommended good eatery. It was a perfect location for us to cogitate over the challenges that lay ahead. I was still determined to continue to achieve my target of getting Boudie to my home at Greyton in the Western Cape. Paps said she was looking at the situation with a sense of 'reality', whilst I was in a mood of determination!

That evening was spent in deep thought and procrastination, ending with us reaching no real conclusion. We were awoken early next morning by the now familiar 'call to prayers.'

We spent a further 'contemplative' day in Ben Gardane. Time, cash and patience were wearing thin, the more we talked it over the more the enormity of the challenge escalated.

At one point I suggested that Paps flew home while I continue alone. While she did agree it was up to me, she threaten to throw Boudie's keys into the desert. She was sure that would be my wife Christine's choice. So, after yet more deliberation, over this **Procrastinating PTI (PPTI),** we decided to ship our beloved hero Boudie back home to the UK from Libya and we would somehow fly to South Africa.

Woken once more by the early 'call to prayer' I was feeling downhearted over the way forward that we had agreed the day before. I was sure I would somehow find a way to continue driving. While we continued to ponder, we chose to spend some time in the Berber area of Tatouine taking in the sights and enjoying the company of the many friendly locals we came upon. A few more days rest would surely do us good, so I booked an hotel some two hours' drive away at the holiday resort of Ile Djerba on the Mediterranean coast. Indeed, it was a wonderful spot, where a restful and rejuvenating weekend was enjoyed. The time was made all the better as we were able to enjoy our first Bubbles and vino for over seven weeks. Progress was further impeded when I took part in an **A**rchery **C**ontest **PTI (ACPTI)**. Having not been near a bow and arrow since I was very young, I somehow managed to win the contest.

During our time at Ile de Djerba I finally, well almost, agreed that the best plan was to ship Boudie back to England. This we could arrange in Libya by putting Boudie on a ship sailing from Tripoli.

As soon as our Libyan visas were issued, we would then meet up with our, compulsory, pre-planned guide at the border.

Plans for Boudie's shipment could be made while we spent time in Libya.

Good news, our Libyan visas had been granted and would be ready and 'active' at the border in three days' time. We had to be there on the day specified as they were only valid for entry on that day. Would I still find the opportunity to change my plans?

Off we enthusiastically went to the Tunisian border into Libya.

Chapter 22
Libya

At the Libyan entry border our visas were granted and entry was gained without any fuss. Libya, as Algeria, demanded we employ the services of an approved guide. This we arranged through a recommended contact that our Tamanrasset friend Claudia had put us in touch with. She in turn got the details from Sam Rutherford, a good friend of hers, who runs an overland, and air ventures operation. Landy-Luck stepping in once more?

We met up with our guide on the Libyan side, this time driving his own car. Clearing Libyan customs was a doddle compared to our recent past experiences, and we were on our way into Libya, after being issued with Algerian number plates for Boudie. We felt that we had finally completed and passed our custom border apprenticeship course! Driving to Tripoli was a challenge as our guide drove like a demon. We soon noticed they all drive that way in Libya. Boudie just couldn't keep up and we had no idea where the designated stop over was to be, other than it was to be in Tripoli. With no other choice we continued unaccompanied on our way towards the city.

Well we got there and once more, by arrangement with Claudia, we managed to meet up with Hadi of Fessano Tours in Tripoli who soon became a very good friend. He was so helpful to us; he found us good accommodation in the centre of Tripoli and recommended sights we should visit; he also wrote-off our 'official' guide. He then introduced us to a couple of guys to help us, as and when necessary.

Spending time in Tripoli was a pleasure, again we found the locals pleasant and friendly. We did travel around Libya in Boudie, visiting Roman ruins such as Leptis Magna, where we overnighted to give us time to take in all we could of the amazing ruined city.

The notorious Roman Emperor, Septimus Severus, was born in Leptis Magna in the year 145. He grew up and fought his way to be the first black African to become

Leptis Magna

Emperor of Rome in the year 193. During this time, he visited Britain, with some 40,000 of his military to 'deal' with the Caledonians.

He strengthened Hadrian's Wall and had many a skirmish with the Caledonians. Septimus became ill in 211, whilst still in Britain; he retired to York where he died. It is thought his remains lie somewhere within Hadrian's Wall. His time in Britain was certainly not as pleasant as ours while relishing in the experience of this **R**oman **L**eptis **M**agna **PTI (RLMPTI).**

Amongst other sites was the ruined Roman city of Sabratha. Once a Roman port, developed from an even earlier harbour, which came to grief, as did Leptis Magna, during some severe volcanoes back in the fourth century.

Sabratha

A recent past resident in the city was Max Hallowan, Agatha Christie's husband. He was stationed there during the Second World War as assistant to the Senior Civil Affairs Officer of the Western Province. During his time in Libya, Max Hallowan was engaged in overseeing the grain rations, while enjoying a comfortable and lavish life style. As we imagined it could have been, during our short and most interesting **R**oman **S**abratha **PTI (RSPTI).**

The recent unrest in beautiful Libya has caused, and continues to cause, far more harm to the people and properties, than all the earth quakes of old ever did.

We managed to visit several areas outside town, witnessing fantastic scenery and wonderful sites. Particularly amazing are the age-old Berber houses built into the hillsides, looking like high-rise apartments carved into the cliff face. I was heartened to witness the many new homes the then regime was building to re-house the Berbers.

All the while we were in Libya, I kept secretly trying to find a way to drive Boudie on to South Africa. I made several enquiries, aware of the well-used east coast route. I went over and over the route I had calculated via Egypt, North and South Sudan, Ethiopia, Kenya, Tanzania, Malawi, to visit an orphanage in Lilongwe, then on to Zimbabwe, Botswana and South Africa. I was happy in my mind, with my new route plan. Visas would be required for the various countries along the way, which I ascertained through my agent in London, were all 'easily' obtainable on entry at the borders. I called up the various embassies to check the situation in each country. First the Egyptian embassy, no problem, next North Sudan, no problem there. My spirits were rising, furthered by South Sudan, they said yes, they would grant a visa on condition we had entry visas for the next country, Ethiopia. My hopes then sank when I was met by a firm 'NO' from the Ethiopian authorities. While they were sympathetic and fully understood my desires, no way could they issue a transit visa as the country had just become embroiled in a state of civil war.

No visas would be granted for the foreseeable future.

The threat of 'the keys in the sand' whacked me again. Sadly, I realised shipping Boudie was the only real choice left to me. Landy-Luck seemed to have abandoned us in Libya as a result of this **E**thiopian **N**o **E**ntry **PTI (ENEPTI)**.

My efforts were now directed toward arranging shipping for Boudie and flights for Paps and me. Hadi found a shipping agent, Mohamed, of Bentraco Logistics who would make all necessary arrangements for shipping Boudie back home to England. For some strange unexplained reason, South Africa was not a shipping option at that time from Tripoli'.

Waiting for information we continued to enjoy Tripoli. Unfortunately driving around, even though we did have local number plates, was quite restricted.

What did I just say about Landy-Luck abandoning us in Libya? A few hours later Mohamed came back advising that it was not possible to ship Boudie to England from Tripoli though she could now be shipped to Cape Town. Well that was better news than expected as Cape Town was the target from the outset. Thank you, Landy-Luck, my Landy faith is now confirmed beyond doubt.

As ever Faith is positive, it encourages things to happen, whilst Hope is merely a wish that things might happen. I now decided to have Boudie 'mated-up' with my Defender110 Kalahari in South Africa. Though Mohamed's following words, "I don't know when we can get a sailing", were not quite so reassuring.

After talking things over with Hadi, he agreed to look after Boudie in Tripoli and ensure her safe boarding if we would like to fly back to Cape Town. I was anxious about leaving, the overloaded, Boudie by the roadside in this busy metropolis, though he assured me she was in safe hands. We agreed, parked Boudie up and booked Turkish airlines flights from Tripoli via Istanbul to Cape Town.

Libya at the time of our visit was a wonderful place to be. Although there was, as people I met at some of the wonderful coffee shops felt, an undercurrent of uncertainty rising amongst the populace. This was just prior to those disruptive activities that split the country into so many factions and flattened many of the new homes being built for the Berbers.

Paps and I flew back, via Istanbul to Cape Town. Back at my South African home, I waited anxiously for news, constantly checking with Hadi and Mohamed who always assured me that all was fine. Some three months later I had a call to say Boudie was on board and about to sail and that she would arrive in Cape Town in four weeks.

I breathed a sigh of relief, though I did wonder in what state Boudie must be by now. Departure was on a Christmas Day. Boudie suffered an anxious **W**aiting **I**n **T**ripoli **PTI (WITPTI).**

Three weeks later I checked on progress to be informed the ship, with Boudie aboard, was docked in Rotterdam.

This, after being told it was not going to Europe! Apparently, it had been loaded into a container deep in the bowls of the ship, so a European off-loading was not possible. I was then reassured the ship would be sailing on to Cape Town.

An unexpected **B**oudie **R**otterdam **PTI (BRPTI)**

The next I heard was from the shipping company in Cape Town that I had engaged to look after affairs at that end.

"Your vehicle has arrived in Cape Town and you need to get there as soon as possible, the customs want to see you".

This was in February; six weeks after Boudie left Tripoli. Christine and I drove to the docks to witness Boudie being towed out of the container. She wouldn't start, was this perhaps in protest for being neglected, or were her batteries flat? With a little encouragement, by towing her around the dock yard with a forklift truck, she was happily resuscitated and burst into life. This reminded me of the day I first started Boudie having recovered her from the hedge in the UK.

The customs officer demanded the keys for the safe under the driver's seat; he was so disappointed to find it empty! Sadly, the Libyan number plates had been removed and I hadn't taken a photograph of them; they were impressive in green and yellow, though meaningless to me.

The greatest surprise was to find Boudie was exactly as I left her all those weeks ago in Tripoli. She had not been interfered with at all; amazingly every bit our paraphernalia was intact. I had left a Tupperware container on the passenger seat loaded with Libyan and other currencies in cash; unbelievably it was untouched! I'm sure Landy-Luck played a leading role in this performance.

We called up Paps, who lived nearby in Cape Town, she took great pleasure in driving her friend Boudie the couple of hours to her new home in Greyton to meet up with her to be new Landy friend.

Landy-Luck was with us all the way.

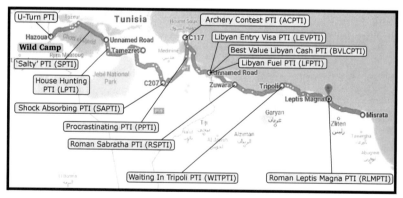

Chapter 23
Boudie in South Africa

Boudie settled well into her newfound South African way of life, it was as if she was meant to be there, being much admired by the Landy loving villagers. Greyton enjoys a healthy colony of 'proper' Land Rovers and enthusiasts. Indeed, it is a hub of faithful Landyites following and experiencing the Landy way of life. Meeting many new friends Boudie soon happily settled into her new village life.

Forward progress was impeded somewhat when helping me out with some home renos and garden landscaping, carrying loads much heavier than those recently experienced during her 'overloaded' overlanding. She coped well, I was proud of her achievements, as were my Landy village friends.

Life wasn't all hard work though. Soon after we were back in South Africa Boudie enjoyed a weekend showing off at a show near Cape Town. This was a fine parade of classic Land Rovers and other classic vehicles on show in Bellville, near Cape Town, where she and others of her breed attracted much attention. Boudie stood proudly alongside a friend's early 1950s Series1' which had spent its early life on the streets of London as a mobile printing press for the London Evening News. Boudie was proud of her weekend on parade during this **L**and **R**over and **C**lassic **C**ar **PTI (LRCCPTI).**

Soon after that Boudie took a weekend off to be yet again impeded at the **C**alitzdorp **L**and **R**over **F**estival **PTI. (CLRFPTI).**

At the Bellville Show

At the Calitzdorp Festival Show

There Boudie, in the company of many of her vintage, also enjoyed some dirt-roading in convoy around the Swartberge Pass.

After so much fun and hard work, Boudie deserved a well-earned treat, so I sent her for a facelift to revive her Land Rover Sand Glow yellow splendour. A two week **M**ake-**O**ver **PTI (MOPTI)** at 'Hot Wheels Health Clinic' was much-appreciated.

Hot Wheels facelift

Time had come to make Boudie more comfortable by doing something about those hard-heavy duty springs fitted before setting out from the UK to carry our overlanding gear.

Apart from the few heavy duty 'landscaping' missions, they were a discomfort now that the rear tub was stripped of the racking, fridge, water tank, cubby holes and other paraphernalia.

Louis Smit of 'Worcester 4x4', also known as 'Desert Stormer', performed an amazing operation using his heavy-duty metal press. He removed the springs, separated each leaf and fed them leaf by leaf into the press, stamping each crosswise at three-centimetre intervals and reassembled them. Hey presto we had a much softer and more comfortable ride. Louis has helped me out many times over the years; that despite his unhealthy addiction to things Toyota.

Fortunately, Toyotaitus is was not catching and though not easy, I forgive him for his wayward drift! He does have a good line of Landy jokes though. Thanks Louis for this **D**esert **S**tormer **PTI (DSPTI)** operation.

Greyton village celebrated a 'Land Rover Heritage' weekend with Local Landy owners bringing their old Landys along to parade for the SA4X4 magazine. Those few more adventurous of us joined Andrew Middleton of SA4X4 with his Heritage model Defender for a spot of 'off-roading' in the, at the time persistent rain.

Boudie - Heritage – Series 1 ready for action

I was among the few to take up the challenge; along with the Series1, Boudie's mate from the Bellville Show, owned by my long-time good friend Richard (Animal). Together we have enjoyed many Landy escapades over the years. We had fun driving over the local hills and mountains, through gorges and rivers.

Once again, it is to my detriment that I recount the following **Off-Road Adventuring PTI (ORAPTI).**

I just had to show-off Boudie's magical talents. The three of us with the Heritage Puma 110, the Series1 and Boudie were attacking a steep incline on a dirt track and happened upon deep 'dongas' created by years of rainwater cascading down the mountainside. Boudie, equipped with front and rear diff lockers, was egged on by me to take the most difficult route through these challenging obstacles. I'm also sure there was encouragement to 'set me up' from some, if not all, members of the group. No problem, after all I've been here many times before. Well that's as I thought, when landing after a mid-air hop, Boudie came to an abrupt halt. Yet again I had arrived at 'Gottenstuk'! I had 'belly-flopped' Boudie onto a ridge in the middle of a donga with all four wheels now suspended high off the ground and spinning merrily with all diff locks engaged.

No problem, Boudie is fitted with a winch. Winch hitched up – oops – we winched the wrong way – stuck even more.

Picture the scene, Animal and I shouting at each other and getting nowhere. A little later another friend, Alistair arrived to help in his Series1. Sadly, with much wheel spinning and the compulsory verbals, we were still firmly stuck.

Yes, you guessed right, it was up to the immaculate, apart from one small dent, Heritage110 to drag Boudie to freedom. Was this a first **H**eritage **R**ecovery **PTI (HRPTI)**? The mission was easily and happily accomplished. Journalist Andrew Middleton commented in the April 2016 issue of SA4X4 magazine: "One can't help giggling at two grown men driving toy-sized 4x4s and getting progressively more bogged down in the pissing rain" Andrew took some brilliant photographs. You may well understand why I took none! Progress was indeed impeded by a **S**how-**O**ff-**O**perator **(SOOPTI),** but the fun for all was accelerated.

The rest the day was spent recounting the happenings and mishaps, with much hilarity over a few beers. It goes without saying that I had to shoulder a degree of some harmless and merry flak that evening!

Thank you, Land Rover and Landy-Luck, for the wonderful 'experience'.

Boudie continues to enjoy her African Life.

Chapter 24

Botswana Puncture

A group of we Greyton buddies spent happy days making our way through the Botswana terrain, having entered the country from South Africa, via the gate at McCarthy's rest. We were driving the tracks doing wildlife and bird spotting. Of course, it goes without saying, we were making the most of the experience by driving Land Rovers.

We happened upon an interesting place for an overnighter, The Rampant Aardvark near Ghanzi, this was our first, of several visits to this great stop-over. It was early evening when we pulled up and pitched camp and supped an early beer while chatting over the adventure so far. A tame Bat-Eared Fox kept us company. There was, of course, much Landy-Life, wildlife and feathery banter.

Mike popped outside to collect something from his Landy, only to discover he had a flat tyre. Great news we thought, another Landy challenge to take on. Fixer and Animal were both excited over the task lying ahead. Within the blink of an eye the high-lift jack was at the ready, tool kits were rummaged through to source a wheel brace, tyre levers and puncture repair kit. The enthusiasm was rapidly coming to the boil. With the Landy jacked up the punctured wheel was off in no time.

Soon jacked up and wheel off

We were feeling good; must be time for another beer. Of course, the tyre had to be partly removed from the rim to get at the inner-tube. Expecting it to be the usual challenge with only hand tools available. It was only then that we realised Mike's Landy was fitted with heavy duty, at least 17 ply tyres, making them extremely tough and rigid. Mike, being a big game vet, rightly felt safer with these sturdier tyres between him and the surfaces he often had to negotiate.

Mike's travels around the bush which presents him with all kinds of **PTI**, in guises that you can't begin to imagine. Once he saved a rhino from certain death by intentionally driving his Landy into its path, stopping broadside in front of the beast as it charged toward a cliff edge. The Rhino came to a sudden halt as it ran into a rear wheel. It shook its head, realising its 'navigational' error wandered off to safety. Mike's Landy was of course undamaged and luckily, he was unharmed.

The drop ahead in the rhino's path was of several hundred feet, indeed a death trap in the waiting!

Back to the puncture repair; after much struggling, grunting and self-lubricating with more beer, the tyre was off the rim sufficiently to extract the tube. Mike, Animal and Fixer were busy finding and patching the punctured tube.

Fixer had his eye on a suspicious Toyota parked close by. We also kept watch for rubber loving hyenas and other furry bystanders. I was once told of Hyenas eating the tyres of planes parked in the bush. One cheeky scalawag once ran off with my rubber mallet, after I had pegged down my tent.

After about ten failed attempts the puncture was repaired, or so we thought.

Time to clear away the glasses

The Landy now standing smartly to attention on all four! It was now time to clear the glasses and bottles away, we then dined and retired for the night.

After a decent night's sleep, it was time to de-camp, pack up and move on. 'Landys to the ready' – Oh dear Mike's Landy has a flat; yes, the same tyre we repaired so many times the previous evening! So, one more repair. I can't imagine why but this time it was a cinch; everything went so easily, all done inside fifteen minutes! Maybe we were now more experienced after our intensive learning curve the evening before! Perhaps Landy-Luck was feeling sorry for us during this **B**otswana **P**uncture **PTI (BPPTI)**.

Whatever, it was yet another great Land Rover 'Experience'.

Puncture repaired, mobile again

Chapter 25
Mozambique

Two Defender 110's and crews, comprising, Animal, Monique, Fixer and me embarked upon another adventure.

This excursion took us the length of South Africa from home in Greyton to the Kruger Park, where we spent a wonderful few days game watching, before entering Mozambique. Approaching the Park at the Malelane Gate, we stopped off to top up with fuel, food and water where we were offered overnight accommodation in some converted shipping containers. It was getting close to the gate closing time, so we decided to give it a go. We were pleasantly surprised at how good they were, like comfortable bungalows inside. Next morning, we breakfasted well in the nearby cafe.

While taking breakfast I surrendered my 110 to a couple of charming young ladies running a car-wash who offered a wash and polish at a very good price. Unable to resist the price, or their charm, they got cracking. The result was a gleaming Defender, in fact I had never seen it so sparkling. However, it proved a mistake as every speck of dust stuck was attracted by gleam and took up residence on the highly polished surface.

It was rather like driving a heavily camouflaged military truck.

Within minutes of entering Kruger we sighted wild life in the form of many crocodiles basking by the side of the Crocodile river, there's a surprise! Of course, the 'Big Five', at least four of them, presented themselves to us as we journeyed north toward the Mozambique border.

We left Kruger via the northern Pafuri Gate. Expecting an easy passage, I was picked on by and overzealous young lady customs officer. For some reason she homed in on my lap-top computer, picking it up she clutched it tight, as if it was about to escape. After some minutes examining it, having opened it up and turned it on, perhaps expecting to see something 'interesting' on the screen, she thrust it back to me. She then made me sign a document to confirm I would be bringing it back into the country on my return, I was then told to 'GO'. What an **E**nthusiastic **C**ustom **O**fficial **PTI (ECOPTI)** send off!

On we went to meet our friends who were now waiting patiently in the 'no-man's land' between the two borders.

Entering Mozambique was, by comparison, a mere doddle. It was not late, but we do like to find somewhere to pitch camp by about four o'clock in the afternoon. We make it a rule not to drive after dark in African countries if possible, so we looked out for a campsite. Following the Limpopo River, we soon found what appeared to be an ideal site occupied by a large crowd.

It looked to be a perfect spot for camping. On entering the campsite, we were immediately greeted, bluntly and quite rudely, by some loud voiced Americans shouting, "you can't stop here". Apparently, there was some sort of religious gathering in progress and outsiders were not welcome.

This helped confirm to me that my faith in Land Rovers is the one to follow. All are welcome to Landy gatherings, any time or place, at a push Toyotorites may perhaps be allowed to join in with us on the odd occasion, provided they behave themselves.

We continued our drive through forests of Yellowwood trees, or Fever Trees as they are known, in the Limpopo National Park. It is alleged they were first named Fever Trees by thirty-six Voortrekkers when making their way south, from Europe, through this part of Mozambique in the early 1800s. They noticed they caught some sort of 'fever' whenever they neared the yellow trees; hence they called it 'Yellow Fever'.

They were convinced they contracted this 'Yellow Fever', when in fact they'd been introduced to malaria by the 'mozzies' living in the low-lying damp areas, where the Yellow Wood trees like to grow. Strange as it may seem now, the Yellow Wood Tree is not the source of Fever Tree Tonic Water, once a cure for malaria when taken with a measure of gin. We all know of Gin and Tonic; popularised by the British Army in the days of the Indian Empire, when it was compulsorily issued as a prevention and possible cure for malaria. No, we didn't take the opportunity to imbibe in **G**in and '**F**ever-**T**ree' **T**onics (**G&FTT PTI**). Gin has been popular for many years, particularly during the sixteen hundred's in London, when it to was so cheap and became known as 'mothers ruin'.

Sadly, in 1836 those thirty-six Voortrekkers were slain under the orders of the notorious Zulu Chief Manhkosi.

Apart, that is from two small children, that were rescued by another Zulu warrior.

Eventually we found a campsite in the region of Mapai in the Limpopo National Park. The location and staff on site, everything was perfect for us. From the moment we drove through the gate we sensed the pride they took, in not just the campsite, but also the environment and protection of the wild life. Most noticeable, was the effort they were putting toward the culling of big game hunting and poaching. It was good to see the number of snares and other trapping devices seized and put on view for all, demonstrating the agony suffered by big and small game.

This we later witnessed at the several locations we visited throughout Mozambique. Not just wild life preservation is important here, but also the re-introduction of the wildlife that was almost annihilated or emigrated during the twenty-seven years of war in the country. Wildlife not slaughtered for food took a run for it across the borders, where they remain and are subjected to senseless savage poaching.

Some seized traps and snares

There was a school at the Mapai campsite for local children, the class rooms were under canvass; of course, they were spick-and-span, as was the outside activity yard area. Pride was oozing out of every member of the team.

The next night was spent at another spotless campsite in the Banhine National Park. The same pride was evident in the staff, who once again were very friendly, helpful and enthusiastic about their work and wildlife preservation and re-establishment.

Our time in this beautiful country was a progressive education for us as well as a great Land Rover 'experience'.

We came across Landys parked up in various states of repair, or disrepair. This provided opportunities to buy several old Landy badges from some of those Landys being broken-up for spares. They make great souvenirs, some with **SA** marking, others inscribed with the old Solihull insignia.

These sightings and badge collecting missions produced quite a few **Landy Badge PTIs (LBPTI)**.

In the UK we continually complain about the potholes in our roads. Mozambique dealt up some enormous pothole experiences. The main tarmacadam roads proved to be more challenging than the minor neglected dirt roads. You soon learn the knack of 'Pothole Diverting', a demanding skill, especially when faced with opposing traffic, the buses and trucks proving real challenges. Those drivers have perfected their diverting skills 'off to a tee'. At any cost they avoid those craters, with an apparent total disregard for whoever or whatever may be coming from either way. I wonder what it feels like to be a passenger on one of those buses, to be swung constantly from side to side and perhaps thrown into the occasional 'crater'?

It was common to see children sitting at the verge of the road with a pile of dirt; most likely excavated from the potholes. As you approached, they would hurl some dirt into a pothole, pat it down with a shovel then hold their hands out expecting a tip for 'smoothing your passage'! With a little better management and some organisation, I'm sure they could make a good living. They would soon be very rich kids if they did the job properly and, of course, if anyone ever gave them anything. Fortunately, as is our normal practice, we avoided the tarred roads as much as lawfully possible so avoiding those enormous **Pot Hole PTIs (PHPTI).**

Potholes are fun on a dirt road, track, or off-road, here on the main highways, they were seriously life threatening.

Why are they named 'potholes'? The Romans, when they ruled over Britain, built very good roads which remained intact once their period of reign came to an end. In those days Pottery was a big business as there were many potters working away, making the vast numbers of pots required. There were no tins, glass jars, plastic bags or tubs, or cardboard boxes in those days. Times got hard, as local clay became in short supply and expensive. Under the smooth cobbled roman roads was a thick layer of perfect clay. During the night-time desperate potters would dig holes in the road to steal clay. Hence the name Pot-Hole; the curse of the waggoneers of the day and indeed remains the curse of drivers throughout the world today, though we can no longer blame potters.

Now heading across the country toward Vilankulos on the east coast. A source of joy happened as we came up to the Limpopo river to drive across when to our glee, we found a Toyota ensnared at 'Gottenstuk' in mid-stream.

Which to rescue first, Landy or Toyota?

Without a second thought we waded our Landys in to rescue the unfortunate Toyotarite from his demise. Parking up on the far bank I took the winch cable, as I was about to hitch up to the Toyota, Animal in his 110 also reached a nearby 'Gottenstuk'. It saddens me to make mention of a Landy reaching 'Gottenstuk', in the presence of a Toyota. Unfortunately, he had unexpectedly found a large hole in the river bed.

Decisions had to be made as to whether to recover the Toyota or Landy first during this **Limpopo PTI (LPTI)**. Another Mozambican pothole.

There were several locals standing by enjoying the commotion as we went about the recovery. One bright spark shouted out "Be quick, they are about to open the sluice gates". He was jesting, or so we hoped.

It must have been 'Toyota Rescue Week', as we soon found another Toyota in trouble experiencing a **C**oconut **TPI (CPTI).**

A farmer with his bakkie loaded to the gunnels with coconuts was unable to make his way out of a field; he was 'Gottenstked' up to his axles. By hooking my kinetic rope to his rear tow hitch we soon had him flying out from Gottenstuk into the roadway and on his happy way.

I was told that years ago the local families were allocated one coconut tree per household to help them survive. It is sad that Mozambique has suffered so many years of war and subsequent poverty. As you travel around you come across many roofless homes, abandoned by the departing Portuguese during the wars. Sadly, they burnt their homes out before leaving so denying the locals any chance of living in them!

We stopped off for several days at Vilankulos, enjoying the sand and sun. Local youngsters would come up from the beach selling very delicious prawns they had just caught; they made for delicious Braais. Also, I bought a couple of lovely paintings from local artists picturing the bay which now adorn my office wall.

Some time was spent beach driving on the vast open shore, though Fixer and I nearly got caught out when the tide came in much faster than we anticipated. This reminded me of an incident many years ago when I loaned my then rally car to a friend to take his new girlfriend for an evening out. They spent the latter part of that evening cuddling up in my car on the beach at Weston-Super-Mare. While they were away in 'cloud cuckoo land' the tide came in; my much-modified Renault rally car was marooned to become irretrievable ending up as scrap.

Mozambique traffic

Leaving Vilankulos we drove south, keeping to the coastal tracks as much as possible, which can only be described as stunning! One overnight stop we made at Pandane, right on the beach, nearly having both Landys visiting 'Gottenstuk' on the way out from the beach area we parked up at. With both Landys at the bottom of the steep sandy upward climb caused us just a little concern as we could not see anything to hitch a winch line to.

There were no coconut trees within winch line distance. In true Landy form and with Landy faith and Landy-Luck both on our side we made good our escape from a possible 'Gottenstuk' or two.

There were no more **PTI** until we hit the town of Xai-Xai when Animal's Defender developed a squeal. Stopping at a

Jockey wheel bearing fix

roadside garage, or was it a scrap yard, Animal found it to be the fan belt jockey wheel tensioner bearing causing a Jockey Wheel Bearing **PTI (JWBPTI).** Landy-Luck stepped in once again as a couple of guys working on some old Landys there jumped our help immediately. Within just a few minutes there was no more squealing. A bearing taken from a scrapper laid-up there cured this minor **PTI**. A CTM to them for their prompt and efficient help.

From then on our drive South was almost **PTI** free.

Apart from the **M**any **T**raffic **PTI**s **(MTPTI)**, in many guises such as accidents, overloaded, slow and broken-down vehicles we came across along the way.

Spending a day and night at the Capital, Maputo, was somewhat different; it was just so busy. The market was quite something.

As much as I tried, I couldn't get away from a young man trying his hardest to sell me a live rabbit he had in a cardboard box under his arm. Wherever I went he followed, with a determination to sell the bunny to me; he failed. The beach outside the hotel where we spent the night looked great, but oh, how it stank of rotten seaweed, if not sewage. For some reason we decided against swimming in the sea.

We left Mozambique, taking with us many happy memories and a determination to make a return visit. I would love to visit the Niassa Reserve north of Mozambique. There Keith and Coleen Begg who, with a dedicated team, carry out incredible work to preserve and re-introduce the wild life lost during those war-torn years. Land Rovers, of course, play an important part in life in Niassa.

We enjoyed many pleasant and happy 'experiences' during our time in Mozambique.

Again, our thanks go to Land Rover and Landy-Luck for having taken us 'by far so far' and for finding us those superb Landy badges.

Yet more Happy African Landy Days and 'experiences'.

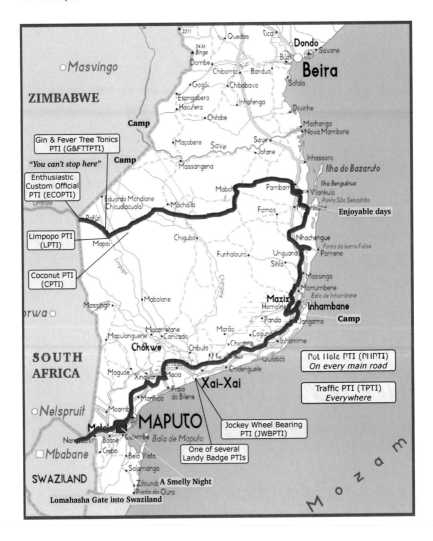

Chapter 26

Swazi-calm

Leaving Mozambique via the Lomahasha Gate into Swaziland was hassle free. Immediately we had a feeling of calm driving through the countryside, looking for somewhere to pitch camp for the night, as time was creeping on.

That night's rest was relished at the Ndlova Campsite in the Hlane Royal National Park. A highly recommendable spot to rest up at. We were more than impressed with the facilities, the layout and cleanliness all around the camping area.

The shining brass water taps on the standpipes dotted around, caught my eye straight away, they were immaculately polished and gleaming. When I enquired why everything was so shipshape and Bristol fashion? "We have always to be prepared for a visit from the King as Hlane is one of his favourite spots" a member of staff replied. *(The word Hlane translates to wilderness).*

The twenty-two-thousand-hectare park is held in Trust by the present King Mswati III, having been established in 1967 by King Sobhuza II to conserve the game and natural resources. The team certainly are working hard toward achieving those aims. Evidence is visible by the multitude of wildlife and birdlife all around. Most prominent are lion, elephant, vultures and marabou stork.

As I am sure the King does, we enjoyed a luxurious Royal night's camping, the food in the cafe on site saw us pleasantly sated and replete making for a tranquil night's rest.

Most of the next day was taken up driving around the well cared for Park, taking in the sites and all the game around us. That one day spent in this calm country was just not enough, another for the list of places to 'go back to'. Time permitting, I would love to have stayed for a couple of weeks.

I really was looking forward to a **PTI**, of any kind to keep us in the Hlane Park, or Swaziland a little longer. I tried but failed to concoct one! This is the first time I recall of Land Rover and Landy-Luck failing to come to my aide when needed.

We left Swaziland after this short visit with a determination to one day return.

Chapter 27

Lesotho Cheese

Back over the border into South Africa, the calls of the now close by Sani Pass were drawing us toward its challenges.

It is a must for any Land Rover enthusiast to drive to the top of Sani into Lesotho, it would unquestionably heighten any Landy drivers LandyLife

Fixer and I, with our over-loaded 110, along with Animal, Monique, their boys Bjorn and Sven in their also well stacked, Ironman, Workhorse110, made for the Sani Pass. This again was in the days before I learnt to follow Jefferson's advice on what not to take on a trek.

Sani Pass

Climbing the pass, rounding its twenty-seven acute bends, was a pleasure, though not quite the challenge I expected.

I must say it was dry, though cold when we visited, so there was no flooding or water-logged track to contend with. Crossing the border into Lesotho was a synch, by simply showing our documents we were in.

Of course, we had to visit Africa's highest Pub, The Sani Mountain Lodge, at the summit. At some two thousand-eight-hundred and eighty metres above sea level, it is the highest point in Southern Africa. Looking back, perhaps the pass was more challenging than I took it to be; am I getting too used to all the passes and terrains I have traversed over the years?

Be careful I said to myself, it's dangerous to become over confident.

It was nearly lunch time as we reached the pub; time for some liquid refreshment and a snack. The menu was impressive, I chose a chicken burger. Drinks arrived, and the waiter politely apologised as they were 'out of chicken'. "I do have some lovely sausage burgers though". It sounded so good that I agreed to dine on their sausages. In no time I was ploughing into a very tasty sausage burger. We continued to enjoy the company and lively ambiance at the Mountain Lodge. We left there, with no real plans as to where were heading for, so set out toward the town of Mokhotlong.

We hadn't gone very far, when I began feeling unwell.

After stopping and discussing the situation, we decided to make for Mokhotlong as quickly as possible. Fixer took over the driving and we followed the Ironman going as quickly as possible on the Lesotho roads, while coping with the driving ways of the locals. With all-speed we were in the town; the first Hotel we found was the Mokhotlong Hotel where we checked in.

Oh, for a bathroom and bed! Looking forward to the comfort of an hotel bedroom, I could not believe what I was hastened into. There was no hot or cold water and the toilet would not flush. 'Jesus' – I didn't quite go mad, but they sensed my needs and soon moved me to another room. This was better in that there was a bed and the plumbing work. It was rather like being in prison, not that I have any previous experience, with bars at the window, the TV was incarcerated within a locked metal cage. The lock on the door didn't work from the inside, so they locked me in. To me right then it was all I needed, 'a loo and a bed'. Monique made sure I was at least comfortable and had everything around me I was likely to need for the next few hours. The staff told us we would be quite safe for the night, as when they go off duty later the hotel doors will all be locked. Did I say it was like prison?

By this time, I was feeling terribly sick and hallucinating.

I had by now suspected the cause of the problem. The sausage given to me at the Mountain Lodge must have had some cheese in it which I didn't taste at the time. Through some weird ancestry issue, I am extremely allergic to cheese. Something I first became aware of as a five-year old at a strict boarding school, where you were forced to eat all that was put before you at the refectory table. Eating cheese brings back the memories of that chastisement by cane and leather strap to this day!

By the time I was released from my jail the following morning my internal system and brain was clear of its problems. We did enjoy a surprisingly good breakfast in the dining room, without any cheese. The staff, given the surroundings, were friendly and as helpful as they could be.

I phoned the Mountain Lodge to check, yes, there was cheese in the sausage; problem solved!

Lesotho, at least along the route we took, comes over as a wonderful country; the scenery, and the snow was captivating to put it mildly. I later learnt that Lesotho is in fact the highest country in the world; 80% of it being above one thousand five hundred metres with a lowest altitude of one thousand metres above sea level. That explained the amount of snow we encountered, enough to make snowballs, which Bjorn and Sven enjoyed throwing at each other; and us.

The locals we met were, again very friendly, mostly dressed in blankets covering them head to toe, and shod with wellie boots.

Living in small rondavels *(round houses),* made from materials close to hand. The walls are often made from stone, the roof timbers from poles cut from nearby trees. The roof is thatched with straw, or other leafy materials, and tied together with grass string. The mortar for the walls and floor comprises a mixture of soil, sand and cow dung which dries out very hard and weather-proof. The more enterprising builders include a layer, about 200mm, of recycled polystyrene food containers crushed and sandwiched between two layers of the walling material. This works well as insulation which is good as it does get very cold in Lesotho. Maybe the rest of the world could learn something from this

We drove through the wilder eastern side of the country, avoiding whatever little tarmac we came across. It was a pleasure, taking in the scenery and watching the locals tending their flocks of cattle, sheep, goats, or driving their donkeys. They were happy going about their day to day business. It was good to see the number of schools that have obviously popped up over the past few years; education is important to them.

Something that took a little while to comprehend were the various coloured flags on poles sticking out of the windows of some rondavels. This I discovered to be the local's way of trading; a green flag indicates 'vegetables for sale or barter'; Red for meat, Blue for fish; there must be others. To warm themselves fires are fuelled by dried cow dung made into brick like logs.

In parts the roads, or tracks, are almost as if made just for Land Rovers. However, we did find a few other vehicles managing to make progress, albeit very slow. One time we came upon a very smart mini bus, packed with passengers and their luggage, stationary in the middle of a bad stretch of narrow track. Thinking it must have reached that now well-known place called 'Gottenstuk' we offered help, hoping to perform another Landy rescue of a Toyota. However, it turned out his progress was not impeded by the terrain, in fact he had run out of fuel. Fortunately, we had of course 'overloaded' with several jerry cans full on our roof racks. Making a gift of some fuel, they were soon on their way. One happy driver and an even happier bus load of passengers; their gratitude rings in my ears to this day. Landy-Luck stepped in to help a non-Landy, a Toyota at that, out of this **Third Party Out Of Fuel PTI (TPOOFPTI)**! You see, the presence of a Landy is good for everyone.

We carried on enjoying each moment of this wonderful country, the many passes, rises and falls along the way.

Sadly, time was running out for us; we had to find the way back into South Africa, so we left Lesotho via the Qacha's Nek Gate. What a different experience from the many Border Gates I have visited around the world. Firstly, there was no queue and we were met by good humoured officials, who looked at our passports, wrote the details down in an exercise book, no computers. They then wished us a good trip and away we went.

Lesotho is another of those countries I intend to revisit allowing more time to explore and absorb the sights, sounds, contours and the friendship of the locals.

I call upon the continuing help of Land Rover and Landy-Luck to encourage these experiences to propagate further.

The return home was most enjoyable as we made our way, again avoiding as much tar as we possibly could. We ventured to Malube onward to Queenstown, Craddock, Graff-Reinet, Beaufort West, De Rust, Outdshoorn, Calitzdorp, Montague and McGregor back to Greyton. Not the most direct route, but interesting, each place en route has a tale to relate sometime.

Once again, our thanks to Land Rover for a mechanical **PTI** free adventure and 'experiences'.

Not forgetting the ever-present Landy-Luck.

Chapter 28
West Coast Wanderings

Fixer, back at home in the UK, was feeling the need for another African Landy-Life fix. With his bags packed, he winged his way over to my place in Greyton to see what could be done by way of a Landy 'boost'. We loaded my Kalahari, this time with a lot less paraphernalia; you see I am learning! Though we still managed to pile in plenty in the way of camping and cooking gear, along with a fridge full of food, Coke and vino. Also, basic Landy tools and needs were thrown aboard.

The chosen route, though not planned in detail, took us north to Hondeklipbaai at the top end of South Africa, on the West Atlantic coast, close to the Namibian border. With the aim of driving back south 'off-road' by the coast where possible, close to but not driving on the beach, other than where legally permitted. I certainly wanted to avoid a repeat of the earlier Namibian brakes' 'misadventure' episode. On the way up to Hondeklipbaai we, of course decided to avoid all major roads, just to make the trip more interesting.

We left Greyton in the direction of Ceres and the Cederberg via Michell's Pass. This pass through the Skurweberg and Witzenberg mountains was planned by Military Engineer Charles Michell, hence the name, and constructed in 1848 by the famed Andrew Geddes Bain. On the way up the pass we followed a 'Tom-Tom bakkie' equipped with antenna and other clever 'bits' doing a GPS survey. Was this the first mapping survey since 1848, or was he lost?

Perhaps I should have lent him Ethel, my Garmin, to put him on the right road without the need of all the clutter he was loaded up with!

It was not until we got to the Cederberg area that we experienced much in the way of what we know as 'proper' dirt roads. 'Good roads' and stunning rocky scenery.

We spotted several **R**eal **E**state **PTI (REPTI)** properties 'with development potential' in these remote areas. It was a shame they were too far from any Shop, Pub and Restaurant, or anywhere else come to that!

We kept going in a northerly direction via dirt roads through the Matjiesrivier area into the town of Wupperthal. The route into Wupperthal used to be a fine challenging dirt road but recently, they had a go at making it into a concrete highway.

It is more hazardous now as the concrete has broken up

The road into Wupperthal

creating a step-like surface, progress was certainly Impeded by this **B**roken **C**oncrete **T**rack **(BCTPTI)**.

Wupperthal was set up as a mission town in 1830, some one hundred years before the town of the same name was founded in Germany. The German town is famed for its efficient overhead mono-rail system. In the African settlement a successful shoe making business was set up to provide local employment and income. Although on a much smaller scale, a shoe business still runs there today which continues and remains the primary, and most popular activity.

We faced a minor **PTI** here when calling into the local store, for Fixer to replenish his now diminished stocks of Coca Cola. Oh dear, the shelves were empty, awaiting the Coca Cola lorry to make a delivery. A **C**oca **C**ola **PTI (CCPTI).**

We continued north on a remarkably smooth dirt road through the Cederberg Wilderness Area, passing many amazing 'Jurassic' knurled rock formations. They look like sleeping monsters from many a moon ago; one noticeably resembled a gigantic sleeping crocodile.

Croc Rock

Onward we went into the Biedouwvallei area where we camped overnight at the Biedouw Campsite; situated off the beaten track, hidden between rocks, trees and fynbos. We were the only campers, though obviously it's a popular and well-used site by parties of hikers, 'expeditioners' and the like, as the facilities were copious and of high standard. Relaxation came easily in this beautiful valley spot. In fact, it was a struggle to decamp and be upon our way the following morning. It felt as if a **D**elayed **P**arting **PTI (DPPTI)** was looming. Should we have stayed for a full day in this peaceful spot? I plan to return there one day. The Cederberg area is renowned for the cultivation and production of the famous Rooibos Tea, which is exported throughout the world.

Once more we were taking in dust from the dirt road going north to Doringbos then on through the Botterkloof Pass.

The surface was not too rough but the narrow track and near vertical drop-offs were intimidating, especially to inexperienced drivers and passengers alike. During icy winters and the wet times, it is advised that two-wheel drive vehicles should avoid the pass. The views from the pass are stunning.

Our target for the next nights camping was the site at the Kamieskroon Hotel, close to the main N7 North/South highway, from Cape Town into Namibia. On a previous occasion, as a party of six, we stayed at the Hotel on the way back from a Namibia expedition. Fixer was with us that time in Namibia when he was introduced to Amarula. We enjoyed a tipple around the Braais in the bush, passing the bottle around on a 'self-service' basis. When we arrived at the Kamieskroom Hotel fixer went up to the bar ordering Amarulas all round. The barman poured and passed the glasses around. Fixer taking one look retorted, "What the F**k is that?". Obviously in a state of shock at the sight of a normal single shot measure; he soon recovered.

The source of Amarula is the Marula Tree which grows in the Bushveld. It goes back more than ten thousand years as a source of food, vitamins and workable timber. In times gone by when a woman became pregnant an infusion of the Marula tree bark was administered to her, one from the male tree would yield a boy or one from a female tree a girl. Should the resulting baby be of the opposite sex the child was considered 'special' as it had defied the gods. The fruit and the leaves are especially popular with elephants that go crazy for it. Warthog, water buck, giraffe and Kudu also very much enjoy a Marula feast.

A game ranger once shared with me an interesting little 'secret'. Find an elephant 'turd', during the Marula fruiting season, break it apart, being dry they easily crumble, inside you will find several Marula nuts from fruit eaten by the elephant. Pick them out, crack them open with a couple of stones, inside each nut is a pure white kernel, pop it into your mouth and chew; it is delicious. I speak from personal experience it is yummy! On second thoughts, it may not be such a good thing to do, as three days later I was in a hospital bed in Durban. I blamed the glass of whisky I was given to wash the kernels down; perhaps whisky and Amarula don't mix, especially as I am not a whisky drinker. I discharged myself from the hospital the next day, much against advice from several quarters and went, feeling well, on my Landy-Way after this **A**marula **K**ernel **PTI (AKPTI).**

After a good breakfast, progress was unimpeded as we hit the road, skirting the Namaqua National park en route to Hondeklipbaai. There we found a good campsite, just behind the Skulpieskraal restaurant where we settled in well. The food and atmosphere in the restaurant were good and the decor interesting. One unusual feature was a bath tub standing on its end converted into a shelf unit, surrounded by wooden trim it looked so fitting. I returned two years later, the bath was still standing there.

Hondeklipbaai, also known as 'Dog Stone Bay', was so named after a rock formation on the coast in the shape of a dog's head. At least it did look like a dog until sometime in 1853 when an ear was chopped off and taken to Cape Town to form the fictitious 'Dog's Ear Copper Company'. During the 70s a severe lightning strike struck its nose off. Today it's not quite the Dog it was.

The harbour was first set up for the export of copper from the then local mines. Today there are two ship wrecks lying within the bay, the Jahleel, a former copper carrier and the once deep-sea fishing vessel the Aristea. With memories of my Skeleton Coast episode in my mind, I decided not to venture too close.

Shipwreck at Hondeklipbaai.

The Jahleel became a wreck in 2003 during a storm, having earlier been refused anchorage at another port. This despite calls to the owner, who was many miles away in Port Elizabeth at the time. When told that Dog Stone Bay could not harbour his ship safely in the ferocious storm, he showed no concern. The Jahleel was sadly left to the force of the raging gales to become wrecked.

The Aristea was commandeered During WWII by the South African Navy when she saw service as a minesweeper. She was returned to her original owners, toward the end of the war in 1944. Not a year later, in 1945 she was wrecked by her then 'too tipsy' captain who was incapable of manoeuvring her.

One brave member of the crew swam ashore, laying out a rope for the crew to come ashore safely. Only one life was lost; I leave you to guess whose life that was?

From here we entered the Namaqua National Park at the northern gate, just along the road from the bay. An official permit is required to enter the Park. The gate was unattended, however there was a notice on a small hut advising: - "Press the button to talk – Release button to listen". Pressing and releasing the button a dozen times to no avail produced no more than an **A**ccess **P**ermit **PTI (APPTI).** With no other option, we made our way into the Park permitless, following the sandy tracks toward the coast.

During a more recent visit the same entrance point was manned by no less than five personnel who all seemed keen to be part of the action. This was just a few weeks after the Namaqua, extremely busy with tourists, spring flower season. It was well worth it; the sandy ways are pure pleasure to follow. Though I must say during this later trip the through roads were very corrugated, due to the very recent heavy, flower spotting traffic flow.

Along the northern end of the coastline we had many admirers in the form of the many Rookeries of seals enjoying life in this breathtaking location. Regrettably though they do 'pong' somewhat; that being their only minor minus point as far as I can tell.

A Rookery of seals

Camping here is pure pleasure. It goes without saying there were plenty of sandy spots to pitch a tent, enjoy a braai and a glass of vino, while resting and watching the sun set in the west. The SAN Parks sites here are great and are well arranged and serviced.

At around eight-thirty on the first evening of our second visit, we were surprised by the arrival of a bakkie with two uniformed personnel. "Are you Martin Smithson?" they asked; well of course I was. I now surmised why there were so many staff at the entrance gate; simply to cause confusion. They had misunderstood, and miscarried, the conversation we had on entering the Park, about us stopping in the park for two or perhaps three nights. If we overstayed our paid permitted time, any dues would be settled at the exit gate. Apparently, the guys at the entrance gate told security at the south gate that we were driving through the park in the one day.

We were now set up in the most northerly camp, Boulderbraai, some 48km which is eight campsites north of their base, at Groenrivier Gate in the south. These guys had visited each site along the coast looking for us. They explained their concerns were for our safety, or perhaps our Land Rover was broken down and we needed help. How could Toyota driving staff possibly make such a suggestion? They were great guys and we much appreciated their concerns. Reading between the lines I really think they enjoyed the exercise and were looking forward to the return trip in the dark.

As we made our way south, we came upon wildlife in various forms, from the proliferous bird life in their various guises and of course many rookeries of seals, a few Meerkats, and the world's smallest Tortoises (The Namaqua Speckled Padloper). Others sadly included a dead Gemsbok by the roadside; too decomposed to ascertain the cause of death, but I don't think it was hunted as the prize antlers were complete and intact.

Further along the coast we spotted in the distance what at first sight, appeared to be a lone white rock on a sandy beach; as if it were a bird resting and pooing spot. Getting closer, we found it to be a dead Southern Right whale. It was huge, some twelve or more meters long; a very sorry sight with its mouth wide open and guts hanging out between its rows of baleen plates. Nearby we found a whale jaw, rib and other bones on the shore line. They are called Southern Right Whales as they used to be the 'right' whale to kill. 'Right' as it swims slowly in the shallow, rock free waters close to the shore and floats when dead; above all it yields copious amounts of oil, bone and blubber. There are only around ten thousand of these species living today. The name Southern refers to the hemisphere it lives in; there is also a Northern Right Whale.

Dead Southern Right Whale

We carried on southward toward the Groen River exit gate. On our previous Namaqua excursion, the officer at the gate asked for our permit, which of course we didn't have, as the entrance gate was unattended and unconnected. After much 'tongue wagging' over the importance of being 'registered' in case of any emergency, he had to confess the connection with our entry point was down. "Sign here and pay" he said, handing me a piece of paper, which I duly signed. We parted good friends and went on our way toward Strandfontein. Landy-Luck was with us all the way!

During this more recent visit to the same gate we were greeted with open arms by very polite and efficient staff, aware of the very recent search party experience. It was admitted the search crew did enjoy looking for us. This generated much banter and hilarity all round.

As before we then followed the trail that passes the lighthouse beside the Groen River, south toward Strandfontein.

One night, during the first trip, we pitched our tent in an empty open barn-style boat house right on the shore line.

It was rather a windy night, so this offered us a significant extra degree of protection from the elements. Once set up I found a door, which I opened to find a built-in table with bench seats in an enclosed room. From there another door led to a plumbed in toilet and wash basin. Though basic, it was like five-star camping for us. We found no trace of the owner, who we would like to have asked permission from and thanked.

Next morning, we had visitors, a local family with a pair of donkeys and cart, they were busy in the local business of seaweed harvesting. They pleasantly passed the time of day with us and went about their work collecting the seaweed swept in by the tides.

I found this barn again during our later meander, hoping to pitch camp, sadly the area is now fenced off for diamond mining with access forbidden. Perhaps the seaweed business will no longer be the main income provider? I hope they consider the locals and their futures.

Our base, the night of this more recent visit, was a peaceful spot very close to the shore where we had a visit from a pleasant retired couple who were passing by. They were on the way from their home in Springbok to their caravan on the coast, which they have had there for some fifteen years.

They certainly picked a beautiful location.

The beach was, as they all are here, vast and inviting you to explore. We were upset to find so much waste of all sorts on the beach, discarded by thoughtless visitors and others filling the sea from near and afar. Fixer and I picked up all the waste we could manage, about three bin bags full which made fuel for a comfortably warming fire while disposing of the waste.

The following day was an amazing 4x4 driving day.

Tyre pressures down, diff-lock engaged and in high range we took up the challenges of sand, shale, mussel-shells, rocks and dirt, with not a sign of tarmac driving. It was 'Landy Heaven'.

Thanks go to Landy-Luck for leading us here and Land Rover

The right sort of road

for bringing us 'so far by far'. Any **P**rogress **T**emporarily **I**mpeded, was of our doing

At last we reached Strandfontein where we camped up at the municipality campsite once again. Almost as creatures of habit, we dined in the very pleasant seafront restaurant. Looking at the menu and copiously stacked plates of food being served up, I asked the pleasant waitress, Sharon, if it would be possible to have a smaller portion. Without a flinch she told me that I could have a pensioner's portion. When I asked what made her think I was a pensioner, she cheekily put a finger on my grey, thinning hair; say no more!

Our first foray of this coastal adventure ended at Strandfontein when we took to the tarmac for a smooth return to Greyton. This time around we explored further south along the coast to Doring Bay, now well known for its relatively new Abalone farming business. I discovered this when trying to find out why so many blue plastic water pipes were piled up all around. They are, I was told, used during the Abalone hatching, rearing and growing process.

It was very quiet as we passed through. The owner of an almost empty store I called into was busy with his staff stacking up a huge pile of Braai wood. "It may be quiet now, but the season is coming, and I must be ready for the tourists" he said. Not finding an excuse for a **PTI** incident we moved on toward Lamberts Bay.

Most of the coastline is decorated with spasmodic large patches of seaweed, collected and spread out to dry.

Once dried it is shredded, or chopped up, and put into bags, ready for marketing. The end-product could be one of several, from foodstuffs, to cosmetics, agricultural fertiliser, Industrial gums, medical uses, or perhaps, how about a seaweed bath? In the bath it is good for rheumatism and arthritis, or so I am led to believe. The world relies on seaweed and algae, as it yields 70% of the oxygen that we need to survive on this planet.

Large areas of the beaches, I noticed, were made up entirely of nothing but many millions of mussel-shells. This, I was led to believe was a relatively recent happening; the empty shells get washed ashore, having originated from places as far away as

Chile. The invasive mussels are carried in by the strong ocean currents to settle on the rocks, breed, multiply and are then gratefully opened and consumed by the local bird and wildlife. Along the shore you find middens where in the past locals would gather and dine on mussels, leaving circular areas of opened shells where they regularly dined. Driving along the very smooth tracks covered in these shells crushed by the many previous vehicles passing over them, I wondered, why not harvest them for covering the dirt roads? A layer of crushed shells makes for smooth comfortable driving, as we experienced driving through them. There is an endless supply, constantly being replenished, along the west coast.

A short visit to a sandy Gottenstuk

This coast is a very popular location for fishermen, professional and amateur alike, as well as the many holiday makers, the casual and more adventurous. Our visits were out of season, best for enjoying the calm peace and restfulness, combined with the sounds of the sea and birds. The sand, rock formations, skies, wildlife and landscapes all contribute to an overall ambiance of tranquillity. The most popular tourist time is springtime,

September-October, when the whole area of Namaqua Land becomes a massive carpet of beautiful spring flowers. The flowers are best viewed with the sun behind you as the flowers face the sun. Driving from North to South, affords the benefit of the best views of the flowers, as they all face north to catch the sun.

The next stop was the welcoming Lamberts Bay, stopping on entering the town at the lovely 'Mad Hatters Coffee Shop' for a break. Parking the Land Rover just outside the cafe I managed to lock it up leaving the keys inside. This was a real case of a **PTI** brewing. What to Do?

Just down the street I found a Garage, the man in charge listened to my plight, laughed and said, "I've got just what you need in my bakiee, follow me". From behind the seats he produced a metal bar, about a metre long with a hook cut into it at each end. "This is what I use each time" he said, "slip it in through the door or window, you may need a screwdriver to lever the door open a bit".

I got the message, wondering how many 'each times' he makes use of this weapon. Armed with the bar I went back to the Landy; fortunately, one window was open by about a centimetre. Threading the bar though the gap and bending it as require, I managed to reach the lock, hooked the bar on and at first attempt it was 'open sesame'. Sadly, this was one of those operator error (me) **D**oor **L**ocked **PTI (DLPTI).**

We then dined and rested in comfort at The Mad Hatters, where we enjoyed good food, fascinating decor and excellent service.

Checking our watches and the calendar it was time to make the long and trouble-free drive back to Greyton.

Thanks again to Land Rover for yet another coastal 'Experience' and for bringing us even further 'so far by far'. Thanks also to Landy-Luck, for keeping us on the right track and for 'opening the door'.

As George Bernard Shaw once wrote, with a small tweak from me:

> 'I never knew of a morning in Africa, *with my Land Rover*
> When I woke up and was not Happy.'

I have to say this is true of all the time I spend in any African country, or elsewhere come to that in a Land Rover, which is never enough for me!

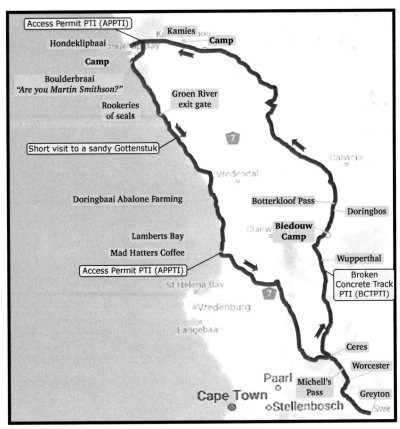

Chapter 29
Boudie moves Home

Life has its little ups and downs. Unfortunately, one time when I was back in the UK, I became quite ill, at the same time one of my daughters was hit with cancer. My condition soon improved and thankfully my strong daughter has recovered. This somewhat reduced my Land Rovering for about a year.

All this time my Defender was being well looked after in the good hands of my friend Schalk Burger. Boudie however was left sitting in my carport at Greyton feeling very lonely and neglected. It upset me to leave her all on her lonesome.

It so happened, through Schalk, I met just the right person to take Boudie into care. Altus Prins, a collector of old military vehicles, memorabilia and tractors. We struck a deal, I sold Boudie to Altus, he agreed I could visit her at her new home and take her for a drive now and again. Altus is a well know exhibitor of his well-cared for collection of militaria. I look forward to attending shows with Altus and Boudie in the future.

Full credit goes to Altus for all the hard work he, and his friends, have carried out on Boudie, she boldly stands out in any crowd, no matter who, where or what the competition may be. She must feel proud, and indeed I am more than happy knowing that Boudie has settled into a new phase of her exciting life. Let the next exciting chapter of Boudie's life begin!

Thank you Landy -Luck for your efforts through Schalk, Altus and friends. Yet another Land Rover 'Experience'. This time it's not a **PTI**, more a case of **B**oudie's **P**rogress being **P**romoted. **(BPP)**.

Boudie in Commando uniform

A while later I had the pleasure of meeting up with Boudie when she appeared on show at the TAFLEBER VETERNAN & ENGIN KLUB show at the Dirtopia Site, a little way north of Stellenbosch. For me it was like a visit to paradise, being there with Boudie and so many Landys and military gear of all ages and stages.

Boudie stood out as "star of the show" parading about, armed, in her Commando dress. There were many attractions such as old tractors, like the ones I drove as a youngster when I first came across Landys and was tempted into a Landy way of life.

There were many fascinating stationary engines, classic and vintage cars on show as well. I was particularly struck by the 1960s Renault R8 Gordinis. Years ago, I had the pleasure of rallying in one of those amazing cars. Another star of the show was a 1901 Benz single cylinder 110hp car which brought back to me the tale of Jefferson and his single cylinder overland trek in 1907. I'll never forget that Benz. While I was standing beside it there was sudden loud deafening "BANG" in front of me. A tyre had burst for no apparent reason. With skill and speed the owners made an improvised repair which worked well.

The show went on, as they say!

Full credit to Altus and his team, not just for Boudie, but also the other exhibits he and his family and friends brought to the show; it was truly amazing. Under Altus, the militaria collection I think would be hard to better anywhere; from jeeps to guns, camouflages and more. Maybe I'm somewhat biased but Boudie stood head and shoulders above them all.

I look forward to more happy days with Boudie.

Also, I must say the display of Landys was most impressive.

This was the Club's first show. I am sure and indeed hope that there will be many more to follow which I look forward to.

CTMs all round.

The weekend was truly a **T**afelberg **V**eteran **T**rekker & **E**njin **K**lub **PTI (TVTEK).**

Chapter 30
Life in Hell

It has been my very good fortune to visit Hell in a Land Rover a few times over the years. My **P**rogress, to Hell, has never been **T**emporarily **I**mpeded, at least not through any Landy quirks. Any **PTI**s experienced along the way to Hell were pure joy. Don't get me wrong, Hell is a captivating place to visit. The journey there is a challenging adventure.

The way down to hell

Contrary to many beliefs, there are no devils, or flames in the Hell that I enjoy visiting so much. Die Hell, as it is called, is a remote rural community, created by a few Boer Farmers during the early eighteen thirties. It lies within the steep Gamkaskloof valley, nestled amidst the Swartberge Mountains. It is thought to have been discovered by those few local farmers when their cattle wandered off through the mountains to this fertile semi-tropical valley. Eventually finding their beasts, they chose to stay and live in the peace and tranquillity the cattle had found there for them. The first resident was Peter Swanepoel soon followed by the Marais, Cordier and Joubert Nel Mostert families. There is evidence of previous life in the kloof, going back to the stone age and the San bushman.

During the Boer War in 1901, some Boer troops entered the kloof finding this hitherto unknown isolated community of some now, one hundred and fifty folks were living in harmony.

For many years there was no road into Die Hell. Amazingly through determination, will power and muscle the locals managed to build homes, a school, which doubled up as a Church, a Honeymoon House' and several farmsteads. Through their combined farming efforts, they became self-sufficient, producing all the food, timber, firewood and clothing they required to sustain a comfortable, contented lifestyle.

Any additional requirements were brought in on the backs of horses, donkeys and by climbing the mountains to the nearest towns of Prince Albert and Calitzdorp, some 20km away.

This included most of the building materials, farming implements and other needs. Resident, Gustav Nefdt, a long while ago, carried, into Hell on his back, a heavy cast iron wood burning Dover Stove. Just imagine the sweat and tears generated carrying that heavy stove for more than 20km.

During the early fifties, some residents bought, and lugged a Morris 8 car over the mountains into the valley to drive on the road they had made within the village.

Of course, fuel also had to be regularly brought in to keep motoring. A few rusty remnants of that car are there to be seen today.

Morris 8 on its way to Hell

The Morris in Hell today

During the late fifties, the enterprising Mr. Koos Van Zyl who, with a bulldozer and the help of eight labourers, set about forging a track the 50km or so from the Swartberge Pass.

The roadway was completed some six years later in 1962. When Van Zyl eventually completed the road to Hell, he met and fell in love with a local girl, they married and lived happily ever after in the valley.

A very steep track, with severe drop-offs, and tight bends, it was and remains, a challenging trail. A sign on the way in advises this to be "Dangerous Road for 48km. "Use at your own risk". A Land Rover 'Experience' in the waiting! They do  say that all Land Rover drivers go straight to Heaven when they die, as they've had so much Hell on earth. That is just not true, go to this Hell in a Landy and you will think you are in Heaven on earth. By the way, the locals are not keen on the word Hell, they call themselves 'Kloovers' or Valley Dwellers.

The views along the way are stunning; as are the flora and fauna, not to mention the Klipspringer which are in no hurry to be out of your way, also the Black Eagles watching over you.

As a visitor it is almost impossible, and indeed maybe sinful, not to enjoy the many **E**cstatic **PTI**s **(EPTI)** to be found in this Paradise on your way to Hell. All combine to make for a wonderful Land Rover 'experience'.

The road to Hell brought many benefits to the locals, for the first time in their lives, they were able to almost pop in and out at will. That compared to the trekking over the previous, however ever many years.

Sadly, the track also brought a negative side to the community as the younger generations gradually left the Gamkaskloof for a broader education and work opportunities elsewhere. As the population left the kloof, the heart fell out of life in Hell; the last farmer left in 1991. Homes and farmsteads were left to fall into decline and dereliction. This is a valley where people lived in harmony peacefully unaware of the Boer War, or indeed the two World Wars.

One ex-resident, Anna was missing the tranquil Kloof life, so in 1998 returned to her old home and farmstead. With the help of family, she set about a restoration project, setting up Fonteinplaas, a fine cafe, restaurant and shop selling delightful home-made jams, marmalades and other home grown and crafted wonders. The restoration added a guest house and a campsite with more following. Fonteinplaas is a museum of how life in Hell used to be. It is now run by her granddaughter Annetjie, who with her husband is continuing with the superb work of bringing life back to Hell.

Anna outside Fonteinplass

Anna's land and dwellings are now the only parts of the kloof in the hands of original family members. Cape Nature Conservation have taken on responsibility for the remaining areas of the kloof. They are restoring, and upgrading the buildings, to the extent they now have water and solar electricity laid on. What would the Kloovers of old given for such amenities?

During one of my drives to Hell, in a Land Rover of course, I called into Fonteinplaas to meet and chat to Anna. Usually we would pitch camp there, however this time being mid-July, the middle of winter, it was freezing cold. Rather than let us camp, Anna offered us the use of the home she was born in. It was so cosy, the beds soft, snug and sleep encouraging, especially as they were shrouded in many layers of eiderdowns.

A surprise in the morning was opening the front door to find the remains of a baboon, killed by a Cheetah for a **Cheetah Dinner PTI (CDPTI)** consumed on the doorstep dining table.

After a hearty breakfast, it was back up the steep vertigo encouraging track, through the valley across the Gamka River, with its 160-degree bends and many hundreds of metre drop offs.

I have spent many happy days in the Kloof, walking the 15km visiting the various old houses and taking in the flora, fauna and wildlife along the way. Many of the old homes have been tastefully restored as holiday lets, helping to bring life and wealth back into the valley. Talking of wildlife, The Animal (Richard) and Monique's roof top tent had a visitor one day when a baboon found its way in; it 'moved' things around a bit, but no damage was done. Other wildlife we met included, Bat-eared Foxes, Monkeys, various buck and many birds filling the air with their dulcet tones.

The name Gamkaskloof comes from the Khosian word Gamka meaning Lion, Kloof of course means valley. The Kloof is some thirty kilometres long by about three hundred metres across.

I will return for more Land Rover Experiences in Hell.

There aren't many Hells to beat it, or that I can imagine one would like to visit. The name, I am sure is incorrect as I call it Heaven on Earth.

Once again thank you Land Rover, and Landy-Luck, for taking me **'So far by Far'** into the **Heaven In Hell PTI (HIHPTI).**

Moving on from Die Hell one time we took the route along the Baviaanskloofberge, running almost parallel north of the famous

Baviaans Kloof. Stopping at a unique camp site, Dan's Den, in the wilderness for a night, a truly rural, basic but unique place to stop. This sanctuary was run by a lovely lady, Julie and her sister. Many thanks to Monique for calling Julie and 'old dear'; she was two years younger than me. What does that mean?

From Dan's Den we followed the dirt roads through Grootsrivierpoort, where we met a young guy on a motor cycle, who in conversation, told us he lived by the river and would not live anywhere else. A little later we passed his home and immediately fully understood his reasoning. What a fortunate young man he was!

Onwards we went to visit Baviaans Kloof another of my favourite places.

Chapter 31

Baviaans

Not far from Die Hell via the lower part of the Swartberge, to the east is Baviaans Kloof, a valley of some four hours exciting dirt-road driving. Formed over many million years, there was but little access through the 200km or so of its length, from Willomore in the west to Patensie in the east. That is until the incredible Thomas Bain forged a road through. This was completed in 1890, it was to be his last road building venture before his death in 1893. Baviaans was the longest one of thirty-two such roads he and his father built in South Africa.

The Kloof road replaces the previous nearby Tulbagh Pass which had been in use for over a hundred years before.

Traces of previous passes are still visible as you drive through. Other passes have come and gone since the 1700s. Of course, mankind somehow made his way through for many years before. It is said there are many spots in Africa where man, as-yet, has never set foot; it's a huge country.

Today the Kloof is variously described as a narrow, steep, winding gravel road, with acute bends, serious drop-offs and liable to flooding, and at times passable only by 4x4 vehicles. It mingles a blend of breath-taking rugged rocky mountain terrain with fabulous views and high plains. More than a thousand different plant species live in the Kloof, including various types of Erica and Protea.

The once thriving wildlife is now returning, thanks to the efforts of Cape Nature Conservation, reversing the past human invasion and decimation of the poor creatures over the past years.

Road liable to flood

Returning residents, amongst others, include Cape Leopard, Buffalo, Caracal, Kudu, Mountain Zebra, Klipspring, Hartebeest, Eland and of course the ubiquitous Baviaans (Baboons) that give the Kloof its name. The birdlife is possibly more intensified here than in many areas of the country. There are more than three hundred species; too many to name but always evident to one's delight, flaunting their colours while twittering in a harmony of tuneful birdsong.

There are no Fuel Stops in the Kloof, so, when arriving from the west we fuelled-up near Willomore at a quaint fuel depot and shop.

Nearest filling station to Baviaans

Entering Baviaans Kloof is stunning as you scale the Nuwekloof Pass, one of the many passes along the way. Rising to over fifteen hundred metres, unfolding glorious views as you make your wonderful way along the dirt road. Baviaans Kloof takes us through the imposing Grootrivier Gorge for some 200km.

My first visit, in my Defender 110, was with my wife Christine, and two good friends, Marlene and Mary. I must add that Christine is not an 'off-roading' enthusiast at all, though she did have a Landy herself back in the UK.

The R332 road, as shown on the map, looks the more direct route to Port Elizabeth, rather than following the well-travelled, tarmacked and boring N2 all the way. At least that is what I told them. This was in the days before Cape Nature took on management of the Kloof, so it was somewhat more demanding then than it is today. Having got as far as Studits, Christine was becoming anxious that we were on the road to 'nowhere'. My attempts to convince her otherwise fell upon stony ground. During this discourse we noticed an entrance into a farmstead.

As my route judgement was being called to task, in we went to enquire about the 'pass-ability' of my chosen route. Meeting the farmer's friendly daughter, she confirmed yes there is a road through the mountains, and that we could get to Port Elizabeth and it was indeed a 'more direct' route. Landy-Luck was with me. My self-esteem was glowing, until she went on to say, "It will take you at least four hours, maybe five or six from here. "If you get into difficulty you can always come back here and rest-up at the farm."

I preferred not to have heard those last few words, as we went on our way, or should I say, my way! As an off-roading addict my spirits were high; but with the now vociferous 'back-seat' drivers my head was 'buzzing'. To me the rises, falls, drop-offs and river crossings were all like dreams come true.

One thing I didn't realise was that friend Marlene suffered from vertigo. The high rises and sharp falls combined with the

A drop off

steep and deep drop-offs, caused her high degrees of anxiety. I leave you to imagine the chat and grief on board I was subjected to as we trekked on our way!

We met one other vehicle, a Toyota bakkie parked up by the side of the track. Hoping to help a stranded Toyota brought on a bout of Landy dominance, thinking a Jap rescue was about to be. No such luck, he had simply parked up to take a walk; how so disappointing. Perhaps he was broken down but just couldn't face the humiliation of a Land Rover rescue!

Should I have done a U-turn to maybe catch him out?

Zig-zag bends

Trailing onwards through the Kloof, watching out for the extreme drop-offs and the severe dizzying zig-zag bends we enjoyed the way through the various passes; well at least I did. Sight-seeing was of little importance to me; my eyes were on the road ahead and my ears, with some reluctance, on the 'verbal advice' from my travel companions. Passes included Nuwekloof at the start, Grasnek, Holgat and Combination Passes. The latter two passes are linked, Holgate steeply ascends then Combination descends even more so and very twistingly so.

We arrived at the end of Baviaans near Patensie inside the predicted four hours. Despite my passenger's angst,

I thoroughly enjoyed my first, of many, Baviaan adventures.

A **V**ertigo **PTI (VPTI)** for Marlene who was very brave, admitting afterwards that she did enjoy the experience.

I have since relished several more 'Baviaan Experiences', some with The Animal and his wife Monique in our two 110 Landys, also other times with Fixer in my Defender 110.

As enthusiastic off-roaders we were disappointed on our most recent foray to find the trail had been somewhat graded, or as I would say 'de-graded' to a smoother track.

More disappointing was that some of the tougher sections have been by-passed. In places bits of the old track are still visible bringing back memories of the past. True it makes the Kloof more accessible to growing numbers of interested tourists bringing some local employment and wealth with them. It is however still a demanding, twisty drive with steep drop-offs. Also, it is a most picturesque route and a joy to be traversing. An awe inspiring three hundred thousand or more hectares of pure unspoilt natural beauty of many variations and vistas.

One-time Fixer and I were tracking East to West from Patensie, approaching civilization toward the Western end,

I noticed a road grading machine parked in a farm yard. This grabbed my attention so much that I just had to drive into the farm to investigate. There we met a most agreeable man, Chris. He readily admitted to not just being the farmer, but also the owner driver of the grading machine. He was pleased to confess that he had been doing a 'good job' with his machine along the kloof. We put our feelings to him, and I immediately re-christened him to be 'Chris de-Grader'; our meeting was in good jest. We parted the best of friends, especially as he pointed us in the direction of a 4x4 track across his and neighbouring farmlands taking us south toward Kareedouw.

I would like to send my apologies to the driver of a white Toyota bakkie, that I later learned was stuck in his driveway as we drove by. It goes without saying that it would have been a great pleasure to have conducted yet another Landy/Toyota rescue.

Thank you again Land Rover and Landy-Luck for introducing me to somewhere that I continue to visit and enjoy.

The 'Experiences' were wonderful.

Chapter 32
Martin Island

Sitting over a braai at The Animal's home in Greyton one evening, we decided a few days Landy therapy was necessary to refresh our Landy devotion. So, what to do? Animal came up with a very good idea, how about a few days in the Karoo with our two Defenders? Why hadn't I thought of that?

The next day was taken up packing our Landys with the usual too much paraphernalia. We all do it, though I must say after past experiences I am now a more lightweight traveller, thanks, once again, to the advice gleaned from Thomas Jefferson. Well packed-up, fuelled and watered-up. We enjoyed yet another pre-adventure braai, followed by a good night's sleep ready for an early get away.

Leaving Greyton we set off north, via Worcester and Ceres, then took the long straight R355 as far as Tweefontein, all the way to the Tankwa-Karoo National Park entering through the south entrance. It was dawning upon me, driving along that long straight road, that we were entering an area of peace and tranquillity, as I have often heard the Karoo described. The road up did get rather boring, being so straight for so far. Of course, the scenery was good, particularly the flat-topped hills, Tafelbergs, spotted now and again. One little **Stinking Dead Cow PTI (SDCPTI)** cropped up on finding a full-size cow lying on the verge. Stopping to investigate, we found it to be well dead and from the stench it had been so for a considerable time.

The Park, an area of some 140,000sq metres was not always so. Apart from an area some 260sq metres, that has for a long while existed as a reserve. The region was farmed by many a sheep and angora goat farmer, who over the years, plot by plot, contributed their land to the Park. As recently as 1998 a farmer, Conrad Strauss, sold his 280 hectares to the SANP, making up the Park area as it is today. The Karoo has been inhabited since early stone-age by the San people who were still there when white settlers came along.

Farming there must have been hard work as every sheep and goat needs some four hectares to survive. Having said that, Karoo lamb is the best you will ever taste, due to the unique vegetation growing there. I'm not eligible to comment about the wool from the sheep or the angora goats but am sure it is top notch!

Our first night was spent wild camping on the bank of the Oudebaaskraal Dam, sharing our time with millions of flying insects, which fortunately didn't bite. The Animal noticed they were attracted by light, so we set up a light on a pole some distance from the Landys, which they kindly hovered around, away from us. We then settled down to a peaceful night in the open. Animal slept on the workhorse's roof rack, I chose to sleep in my sack on the ground; no crocodiles here! The stars were amazing to gaze at with their brightness and clarity without a hint of light pollution in

The animal at rest

the sky; it just didn't look real! Now I understand why the world-famous observatory is at nearby Sutherland.

We awoke to find many companions dropping in. Hundreds of Pink Flamingos landed, some squabbling, others feeding but most just standing around on one leg. I tried to compete to with them by 'outstanding' them on one leg; of course, I failed This was a **O**ne-**L**egged **PTI (OLPTI).**

Maybe our pink feathered visitors thought us not to be good company, or was it something I said, as they soon flew off to waters new. Their companionship was enjoyable, though after a while a familiar 'pong' started to waft up my nostrils.

Where I live in the UK, I am fortunate to be near the wonderful wetland and bird sanctuary, Slimbridge Wildlife Trust, established by Naturalist and Artist, Sir Peter Scott. Among the vast resident and visiting birdlife Flamingos reside in considerable numbers. Visits to Slimbridge introduced me to the 'Flamingo pong' now wafting back up my nose in the Karoo.

Once our new-found friends had departed, we enjoyed a hearty 'Animal' breakfast. Landy-Luck suddenly brought an opportunity to my notice right in front of me, an island in the dam! I took my chair and waded out to the island and staked my claim, naming it 'Martin Island' were I lounged in a **M**artin **Is**land **PTI (MIPTI).**

Martin on Martin Island

Many designs for a flag to reveal my sovereignty were going through my head, of course it would have to feature a Landy. But then it dawned on me the island was somewhat on the small side and I would have to park my Landy on the mainland overnight. After thinking it over I realised that neither SANP, or the local planning office, were likely to grant me planning permission to build a house and garage on this heavenly island. So we de-camped and continued our Landy-Life retreat on the Karoo mainland.

Following the tracks through the Karoo there are several gates, which always, in true off-roading manner, we left as we found them, which in nearly every incidence was closed.

Our meanderings took us mostly to the north through Langkloof and beyond to the Watervlei area. Looking for somewhere to set up camp for a night, we selected a spot beside a derelict one-time farmstead in a kloof. It was another very quiet, peaceful and restful night, though there was a troop of Baboon nattering away in the hills around us. I'm sure they were just gossiping about the travellers that had just moved into the farm below them; wondering what crops they might plant for them to raid.

It was so very quiet, we saw no one. Ending our visit, we realised we had traversed a few 4x4 trails, such as Leeuberg and on our way out the Watervlei trail. They were appealing and not over demanding for our Landys. We did however for a while get sort of lost at the top of The Watervlei, where we found ourselves going around in circles trying to find our way. We eventually found the Gannaga Pass, quite spectacular, which proved a suiting farewell to our Tankwa retreat. Our Landy commitment was certainly reinforced, especially as it was mechanically **PTI** free!

Thanks again to Land Rover and Landy-Luck for yet another great Landy 'experience'

Chapter 33
Some UK Off-roading

I spent many a weekend off-roading at various sites in the UK with Landy friends. One such site was amidst the Welsh hills, not far from Rhayader that was regularly frequented by a good number of we keen off-roaders. Known as 'Tommy's, it was on a Farm, run by 'Tommy' and his wife, it was a challenging and very popular site on about sixty acres of hill farm. The terrain ranged from smooth undulating meadow land, well there was at least one meadow, two rivers, deep gorges, welsh mountain sides, valleys and waterfalls. Not only an amazing site for we Landyites, the setting and scenery was also stunning.

One very steep hillside, known as The Widow Maker will never be forgotten, especially by my friend Fixer. One time, while descending that steep incline he missed a gear and before he knew it his Landy slid, then rolled over many times, down the long precipitous slope. Fortunately, he was thrown out of the cab as his Landy continued to roll many more times, all the way down the hillside. Sadly, Fixer broke his back but, after some time, he was lucky to make a good recovery, as did his trusty Landy. Despite this set-back, he has not lost his enthusiasm for all things Landy. He keeps a video of the event, to remind him of how extremely lucky he was. Landy-Luck was surely there for him at this **Widow Maker PTI (WMPTI)** spot. Fixer continues to enjoy off-roading days, whenever and wherever possible.

Over the years we have visited and enjoyed countless days of camping and 4x4ing at 'Tommy's' farm. Most of my visits were in my Hybrid Landy, named Chloe. She was a Range Rover on a shortened chassis, with a '90 cab and front end and a Series tub at the rear end. Power came from either a V8 or a 300tdi, changeable at a whim. 'Add-ons' included a winch, steering guard and various suspension lifts from time to time, along with springs and uprated shocks. ARB diff lockers were fitted front and rear which more than proved their worth many times over. A roll cage and rock sliders were fabricated to fit as were many other necessary, and of course unnecessary bits and bobs, as one usually does. Most of this work was carried out by good friend, Bryn Hemming in his workshop near Tewkesbury. Bryn was a one time UK winching champion.

Arriving at Tommy's for a fun day out

A great guy, but now sadly out of the business and Landys, to follow his pursuit of other interests. I thank Bryn for all he did for me in the past on my several versions of hybrids and other Landys. Perhaps, one day he might be back in the business.

Sadly, Tommy's site became just too popular as it attracted too many of the wrong element; those interested more in drugs and disorder. They destroyed vehicles on site, the site itself, the countryside and caravans left there by frequenting weekenders.

It was so sad for Tommy as he was eventually forced to close his wonderfully challenging site for all the wrong reasons.

During all the times we spent at Tommy's the only **PTI**s Chloe ever encountered were caused when visiting the now well known 'Gottenstuk', or tipping over and the like; much as expected really. I recall one cold February day when I tipped Chloe over in a river for a **C**old **W**et **R**iver **TPI (CWRTPI).**

With the help of the ever present Landy friends, and a dose of Landy-Luck, she was righted with no damage done. I carried on my cold wet-way to enjoy the rest of the day; thankfully there was a heater, of sorts, in Chloe.

One time at Tommy's, four of us, each with our Landys, were at the top of a steep escarpment assessing the possibility of making it the hundred metres or so to the base and back.

It being so steep and very wet, with no other way out, other than back up the slope, we opted against the near suicidal attempt. We were about to board our steeds when a toy Toyota steamed past us straight down the incline, very quickly making to the foot of the sheer drop. Fortunately for the two lads in the Toy, they were the right way up on arrival. Try as they might, they could not make more than a couple of metres out of the demise. What to do? We could not afford the risk of sending one or more of our Landys down the slope only to meet the same fate.

We were determined to prove the Landys superiority over the Toyota. We bound two of our Landys together on the flat at the top, as an anchor point, then joined Fixer's 110 and Chloe together with their winch ropes. The two were slowly winched down the slope as far as the winch from one of the Defenders would allow. Fixer's 110 was then anchored at the near max limit of the first winch cable. Fixer then let Chloe down on his winch rope, again as far as possible, where she was likewise anchored. From there we pulled my winch out as far as it would go, which still was not far enough to reach the now very concerned Toyotarites. Having let out some 80+ metres of winch cable, we were still some 10m short of our target. Fortunately, we had Chloe's 5-metre tree strop and a couple of seat belts which, added to the winch cable made up the shortfall to reach the stranded Toyota. Hitching one of the seat belts to the Toyota, we very carefully winched it the short distance of the two seat belts, then un-hitched and re-hitched to the strop. This process was repeated until the Toy was at the end of Chloe's winch cable. With the two anchor Landys at the top, my friends managed to winch the Toy and Chloe a few metres further up so we could block the Toy and unhitch and re-hitch up. With three winches now pulling we all slowly made it to the top of the escarpment. The nervous Toy, and all we Landys slowly crept up and out of this very dodgy situation.

There were two very relieved and happy Toyotarites after another **L**and **T**oyota **R**ecovery **PTI (LTRPTI)**. No damage was affected upon vehicles, people or landscape.

Travelling to and from sites, when not trailering, brought on a few **PTI**. Once driving Chloe back the hour and a half to my home, all was going Landy well until I was passing a large truck when I heard an almighty bang. Suddenly I, and the truck, were engulfed in clouds of black smoke. I was driving quite quickly, possibly too quickly for an old Landy, when the sudden loss of vision was more than a little scary. I soon found the truck driver was in the same predicament. Fortunately we both, without panicking, slowed down, pulled over and came to a stop, avoiding colliding into each other.

The very local black clouds pointed to the cause of the problem. The turbo bearing had ended its time on this earth. Engine oil was pumped out on to the hot exhaust manifold, catching fire and creating thick black clouds of smoke making for a **S**mokey **T**urbo **PTI (STPTI)**. I had a fire extinguisher on board, but the fire soon burnt out once we had stopped, fortunately without any further damage, apart from a few burnt rubber pipes.

The truck driver soon recovered and went happily on his way after offering whatever help he could give us. It was along way for Fixer to tow Chloe back home on a Sunday evening. Needless to say, we made it to home without any further **PTI**.

Another popular trail is the seven mile long Strata Florida, again in Wales, as were many of the green lanes we travelled over the years. The route was well marked out and maintained. Hopefully, with responsible off-roading, it will be kept that way for years to come. Strata Florida is particularly appealing and, at times challenging; even more so during the wet times, due mainly to the number of challenging water crossings along the way. They must always be approached with caution and never be negotiated without other off-roading buddies around.

Sadly, in September 2008, during Strata's wettest time for many a year, seventeen year old Louise Ferreira lost her life there. Louise was a passenger in a Land Rover as it attempted a flooded river crossing. The Land Rover was swept away drowning Louise. Two other Landys in the convoy made it safely across. The driver was later jailed for causing Louise's death. We all have to learn to be attentive, take the conditions into account, be careful and prepared not to take avoidable risks, especially when other lives are in your hands. There is a memorial to Louise at the spot to this day.

In North Yorkshire, in the Langdale Forest, there was once a first-rate 4x4 site. Under the name of Langdale Quest, a well set out, well managed and monitored, challenging site.

Off-roaders were on site for rent, should you wish to save your own chariot from damage. Many did so.

The course was clearly marked and mapped out, signposted; very helpful for finding your way through the pine forest. One draw back at certain times of the year were the swarms of resident mosquitoes living in the forest that were constantly looking for blood supplies. Never to be forgotten were those nights camping with much swatting, spraying and cursing. I am sure they waited for us, they certainly had many a fill of my blood. They do say it's only the pregnant females responsible for the agony. There must be a lot of pregnant mossies about!

Only once did I drive my Chloe all the way north to Langdale, other times I trailered her there behind my Disco3. One time, when I had driven to the site, 'Murphy's law' put in an appearance. While I was having great fun traversing rocks, deep mud and water, side slopes, huge craters and more, I managed to break a steering bar. Chloe became cross-eyed, or cross-wheeled, making further forward progress impossible.

Well, Landy-Luck was with us as friend Bryn, happened to be in our party with his Landy, in which he had some welding rods. Taking the twin batteries out of the Chloe, Bryn linked them together and connected jump leads. We aligned the wheels and married up the ends of the broken steering arm. Bryn, being the expert welder we know him to be, set to and welded away. Within just a few minutes and much welding, while holding an Allen key over break as reinforcement, the flashing was soon over and all was welded up and straight. It was an amazing welding experience to witness. After a brew, or some other liquid refreshment, all had cooled down and Chloe was once again restored and raring to go.

Finishing the course, without any further incident, apart from a few enjoyable visits to 'Gottenstuk'. I drove Chloe, in convoy, with my Landy friends all the way home to Malvern.

A few days later a minor operation was performed bringing Chloe's steering back to fighting fit.

A **Steering PTI (SPTI)** through no fault of Land Rover.

Many thanks to Bryn and, of course Landy-Luck.

Some Langdale memories

Chapter 34
It's a long, long way to Zambia

On this occasion, when back in South Africa, six of us set out from Greyton for a trip to Zambia. Driving two Land Rovers, my Defender Kalahari and another DefenderTd5, a twin cab, belonging to friends Les and Caroline. We were joined by their son Ollie, my granddaughter Amy, and Fixer making up the six.

The first couple of days were hectic to say the least, though we did manage to make a stop at the Lord Milner Hotel at Matjiesfontein for a brunch. This history laden hamlet is in the wild Karoo, encircled by mountains. The settlement was created in the early eighteen hundred's by Scotsman, James Logan. Originally, he had come from Scotland to work for the newly built railway from Cape Town to Johannesburg and beyond, famous for the 'Blue Train'. James saw the need for a rest and refreshment area to meet the needs of passengers, as the train stopped for fuel and water at the then new Matjiesfontein Station. In those days there were no buffet or restaurant cars on the trains.

Under his supervision, in the 1890s the two-story hotel was built. Before completion the hotel was commandeered by the British as a hospital during the then Boer War. Some 10,000 British military were encamped in the vicinity for the duration of the hostilities.

So much history, as can be realised by visiting the War, Railway, Motor and Victoriana museums at Matjiesfontein. Many famous personalities have stayed at this Hotel which was named the Lord Milner in 1970; now a National Heritage Site.

I was told that Queen Victoria once laid her head down in

the best room in the house, as did Lord Randolph, Winston Churchill's father. Amongst other guests were Cecil Rhodes and Rudyard Kipling.

Another visitor, lawyer and author, Olive Schreiner famously commented:-

"It is curious, and to me very attractive
this mixture of civilization & the most wild, untamed freedom;
the barren mountains & wild Karroo & the railway train."
(Olive Schreiner, March 25th, 1890)

This was not all gleaned from the time of our breakfast stop, I have stayed there a few times, though I don't rate among the many famous patrons of the past. One time when Christine and I stayed, there was no water in our en-suite bedroom. Mentioning this at reception, I was told that the water was off for now as there were 'black bits' in it. Taking the opportunity, I went next door to the Laird's Arms, where I was delighted to see there was beer on draught. Asking for a cold pint the barman told me the beer was off for the moment – "There are 'black bits' in it" he said. What do you read into that?

Allow Nelson, the very amiable butler, to show you around and take you for a ride around on the old red London Bus.

It's a laugh, that is if there are no 'black bits in the fuel' and if it starts.

We are still a very long way from Zambia. On we go, through the Karoo, passing the observatory town of Sutherland, the coldest area in South Africa, not that we noticed as we hurried on our way north.

That night we enjoyed the luxury of a bed at the Riverside Lodge in Prieska, south of the Orange river, in the Northern Cape. It had been a long day, sleep came the moment my head hit the pillow. Rest was a must as we had a long way to go next day, our target destination being Tsabong, across the border in Botswana. This entailed covering one thousand and more kilometres to reach the McCarthy's Rest border crossing point into Namibia before it closed at six in the evening.

We made it to McCarthy's just before closing time, stopping on the way only to brew a coffee and sip a cuppa soup. Much to the disappointment of the younger crew members who were expecting a stop off at a KFC we passed earlier.

Thank you, Landy-Luck, for a smooth and **PTI** free day. Crossing the border into Botswana was simple and trouble free.

During the evening we enjoyed a sip and a braai followed by a well-earned comfortable night's sleep at Berrybush Farm.

It was here during an earlier visit, we experienced, my late friend Stuart's, **B**otswana **C**lutch **PTI**. The old clutch plate was still where we left it, leaning against a wall, more than a year earlier, thinking it may have been useful to someone.

Next morning, after a minor **P**uncture **PTI (PPTI)** we popped into the now familiar shop with the two petrol pumps just down the road, where we topped up our tanks, victuals and got some local cash, Pula. The Botswana word Pula, bizarrely translates into English to water; isn't that just how money is spent?

Progress from now on was somewhat slowed by not just dirt, but sandy roads, we are now in desert terrain. On our way to the Mpayathultwa Pan Camp in the Mabuasehube reserve, on the eastern side of the Kgalagadi Game Reserve.

Our map showed an easy jaunt of about one hundred kilometres, it looked an easy day ahead, enjoying the sand roads and spotting wildlife as we go. The roads are indeed 'sandy', just as I enjoy them. Caroline later said that it was like playing Wacky Road Racers, watching my Landy doing its thing in the sand.

We spotted much wildlife during this short trip, including a mother Cheetah with her three cubs lying in the road. They scurried off into the scrubland on spotting us. We waited a while hoping to see them reappear; of course, they didn't.

Just another Botswana main road

Getting to the campsite during mid-afternoon gave us time for a late lunch and to pitch our tents. We lazed at a nearby water hole enjoying sun-downers while watching the local four-legged friends come to sip their refreshing drinks. Amongst the gathering were Wildebeest, Springbok and Jackal. The bird life was also very active, having a happy time singing, bathing and drinking.

Our sleep that night was abruptly disturbed by a Lion that came to within about a meter of the tent in which Fixer and I were bedded down. Mr. Lion made his presence known by roaring his head off right outside, making the tent shake while terrifying we mortals inside. Fixer asked, "what do we do now", I just whispered "Shut up" (those were not my actual words). After about twenty minutes of the Lion serenading, he ambled off, or at least I guessed he had, there was no way I was going outside to check. Those were a very long few minutes; it seemed more like hours to us.

Strange, but we were up bright and early next morning when the hub of conversation was last night's Lion 'serenade', and of how brave we all thought we were. Bravery is so easily hatched after an event! Someone later mentioned that Lions possess the world's most efficient can openers; referring to their 'claws'. Just a stroke to the side of your tent rips it open for them to enjoy a fulfilling fresh human flavoured dinner.

This could have been a **Lion Tin Opener PTI (LTOPTI), or** worse.

Looking forward to more sand driving we continued our way toward Ghanzi, some three hundred kilometres to the north. Before hitting the sandy highway, we went Lion hunting. There, sitting amid long grass we caught site of a lone male lion with his eyes on the Landys. Was he the soloist of last night I wondered? He moved closer to us, then sat himself down again, he was looking around, then other lions came rolling down the slope toward him and the waterhole near-by.

They came very close to the Landy, there were now a total of fourteen lions frolicking around.

For a moment it looked as if a fight was brewing between two females, but they were just greeting each other like long lost friends. A **Lion PTI(LPTI)** enjoyed by all, Lion and Man both.

Drifting along the sandy roads, we enjoyed, not just the sights, sounds and sand. One sound I would rather not have heard came to my ears, rather like a 'sand-worn' front wheel bearing in pain. Of course, a spare wheel bearing was not included in the heavy ammo box of 'just in case' spares I had on board. It didn't seem too bad, so we decided to keep going towards Ghanzi for the night, then tarmac it from there to the Land Rover Garage in Maun. That's the same garage Fixer and I visited during our Botswana Steering experience. We stopped for refreshment and fuel at Hukuntsi, the only fuel pumps we could find, then on to Ghanzi. After a sleep under canvass we hit the tarmac once more the couple of hours to Maun. At the garage we were met with open arms, recalling the time I called in with the V8 Disco1. Problem identified they set too and soon fixed the **S**and **W**orn **W**heel **B**earing **PTI (SWWBPTI).** We were Landy rolling once more!

Moremi Wildlife Reserve was our next planned stop. Sadly, we were unable to make an overnight booking as we were too late, so we arranged a drive through for the next day. The Kaziikini campsite site, just about twenty-five kilometres south of the Reserve, took us in for the night where we Braaied, relaxed and slept well.

I can only describe that day in Amy's own words, from her journal about her first visit to an African Game Park:

"WOW!
That's about all I can say about today.
It was amazing, we saw a lot of game today.
We saw a giraffe then lots of impala and deer type things.
We found elephants and hippos in the rivers.
In the long grass we saw warthogs running with their tales held high.
A zebra and a herd of giraffe followed by more elephants"

What more can one say?

Recent heavy rains had spawned some wonderful mud-holes and fords to splash our way through. One time the road ahead was well under water, it looked too deep, even for a Landy to navigate. Wading into the water to nearly waste height I decided it would be too risky to ford, especially with passengers aboard. Taking a de-tour around the edge of the water we hadn't gone

more than a couple of hundred meters when, resting at the edge of the water were two crocodiles. Was I glad not to have been in the water just there?

This **F**lood **PTI (FPTI)** could have become a **C**roc **F**eed **PTI (CFPTI).**

Being me, I take my preferred route when possible, it's my 'muddy way'. On the way to Zambia we arrived at 'Gottenstuk', only twice for the winch to be activated. Once for

Once more at Gottenstuk

About to become Un-Gottenstuked

me and once for Les. It's always good fun to winch a Landy and to be rolling again on all four wheels.

All part of fun winching **G**ottenstuk and **W**inching **PTI (GWPTI)**.

We hadn't gone very far when we met up with a well renovated, preserved and converted Forward Control Landy taking a group through the Moremi Reserve on a of safari tour. To we Landyites it was a fantastic spotting, perhaps even more so than meeting a Cheetah in the road; certainly the FC was a much rarer sighting.

Sally, the Forward Control Landy

That night we pitched camp, at the Toro Safari Lodge. Our tents will never go there again.

We are now close to the Zambian border, with just the Caprivi Strip in northern Namibia to cross. The girls had some Pula left in their purses which need to be 'leaked' before leaving Botswana, and we didn't want them to wet their purses! While they aimlessly shopped, Les, Fixer and I took the Landys to the local filling station, fuelled-up, topped-up the jerry cans and checked all the levels.

Now at almost the most northern tip of Botswana we crossed over into the Caprivi Strip at Ngonga. A pleasant and simple procedure led us into Namibia for the short sixty-five or so kilometre drive to the Zambian border.

Once again thanks go to Land Rover, for the 'experience' and for having got us so 'far by far'.

Landy-Luck of course played her part.

Chapter 35
Zambia Zest

Entering Zambia through the Katima Mulilo Gate was like a comedy act. There were several desks to report to, each for one thing or the other, we had no idea what, or where. Just another lesson to be learnt before completing our now extended border crossing apprenticeship.

Not knowing exactly what, or where to present ourselves, our vehicles, goods and any other papers they felt they would like to examine we just bundled along. The desks, for want of a better description, were first in a building, then we were sent to a garden shed, finishing up in what appeared to be an old caravan. The scene inside the van was hilarious, the table was on a forty-degree slope, next to it was an old sofa upon which a member of staff, or someone, was stretched out. A mattress was also laid out on the floor; perhaps more comfortable than the sofa. The van was brightened up by a Mr. Whippy ice cream poster stuck on the wall. The service, though unhurried and long-winded, was friendly and welcoming, we were happy to be in Zambia.

The Liuwa Plains was our targeted destination to the north; true Land Rover territory. The main road from the border was horrendously bumpy and littered with deep dongas to cross or circumnavigated. The sightings of the mighty Zambezi River to our right more than made up for the 'shake rattle and roll' we were experiencing. We just had to rest up now and again to take in the view and serenity surrounding us; also, to allow our joints to recover from severe corrugation-itus.

One time we met a local family with a twelve-month-old baby playing by the river, Fixer had with him some of his granddaughter's old baby clothes to give away as a **L**ittle **C**haritable **PTI (LCPTI)**. The happy family were delighted with the gifts.

Choosing to camp for a couple of nights by the Zambezi river we pulled into the Kabula Lodge, a heavenly spot right on the river bank. With tents up, it was time for sundowners, which we enjoyed sitting on a veranda, watching the rolling waters go by. We made up our minds that we were most definitely spending the next day at this heavenly spot. I'm sure the Landys would also enjoy the extra **L**andy **R**est **D**ay **PTI (LRDPTI).**

Kabula Lodge

Fishing seemed like a good idea in the morning, so we took a boat and tackle provided by the Lodge and 'off a fishing we went'. Before casting a line, we met up with a family of hippo and a couple of crocs lazing in the waters. Rather big fish me thinks, not sure we'd get one of those on board our little boat.

After nearly an hour, I was the first to get a bite. Reeling the line in the 'enormous' tiger fish nearly makes it from the hook to the net. Would you believe it, the biggest tiger fish ever got away'!! Amy had more luck, her tiger was jumping out of the water at the end of her line, it got very close to the net, but managed to escape at the very last moment. Boating our way back to the lodge Fixer caught a beautiful tiger fish, weighing in at 2.5ks. This lucky, beautiful, tough and thorny tiger was released to be back with its friends and family. How often have you suffered listening to - 'the ones that got away fisherman's tales'?

Later that day we enjoyed a sundowner, boating up the Zambezi, the Hippos, Crocs, sunset and views were stunning. An amazing **F**ishing and **S**undowner **PTI (FSPTI)**.

We befriended Kennister, a gentle chap working at the Lodge, he took us up the road to visit his village. It was a pleasure to see how happy and contented everyone was. Kennister showed us everything in the village, his house and how they live.

Kennister showed where and how they grow veggies and animal feeds; the livestock, how they tend them; the stores, for the harvested crops, for their use and for the livestock. It was as

Kennister's village

if they were one big happy contented family. Kennister then took us to a friend's remote village, not far away. The trek there was right up our street, there was no road as such, just a fun drive through the trees.

Les related the tale of the Mopane trees, with leaves shaped like butterflies, as we passed some by. Long ago the butterflies were unhappy and complained to God who asked them why they were so unhappy. "Because the monkeys keep eating us" they said. So, God planted the Mopane trees with leaves shaped like butterflies for the monkeys to happily feast upon instead.

Again, thanks to a **H**appy **K**ennister **PTI (HKPTI)** we found another calm and peaceful community getting on with and enjoying life. Indeed, much as how life should be.

We carried on Landying our way along the dusty bumpy road toward the Liuwa Plains. We stopped off to visit the Ngonye Falls, just a few minutes' walk from the roadside. The falls impressively demonstrate the power of the mighty Zambezi River as the waters cascade powerfully over the rocks.

A little further along the road we came across three locals, working on their, apparently, broken-down car parked at the side of the road. With the bonnet up and the front fender hanging

off, the 'team' gave the impression of being in difficulty. Two of them waved us down asking for some fuel. The scene had been set up as a scam, with the car placed as bait to entice the likes of us to stop and offer them help. When questioned, they readily admitted the scam, telling us they had been there for three days, stockpiling fuel donated by 'helpful' passers-by poured into containers they had with them.

As they were such likeable scallywags, we also left them a small measure of diesel to boost their ill-begotten gains. I'm sure they later sold on most of the stockpiled fuel at discounted prices.

Not far from Sitoti we crossed the Zambezi by ferry. The roads were now in a terrible condition, floods had washed away the bridges and much of the roadway, though I must admit it was like heaven for we Landyites.

Washed away bridge and road

We were now in the region of Barotseland, an area that kept its independence during the colonial times. The locals are the known as Lozi who are led by their Litunga (King); currently His Highness Lubosi imwiko. When the annual floods come, the

King and his followers evacuate the region in barges during a ceremony called Kuomboka, which literally translates to 'get out of the water'. The Litunga leads the procession in his black and white striped, well loaded, garnished and manned barge carrying a full-sized effigy of an elephant on the cabin roof. With much banging of drums, singing and dancing they sail in convoy from their homes in Lealui east to Limulunga in the higher plains. The process is repeated when they sail back as the floods recede a few months later.

We didn't have the pleasure of seeing the ceremony as we were there during August, though we did get a glimpse of the Kings boat awaiting the next Kuomboka. The annual floods occur during January and February causing havoc each year, as is apparent by the state of the roads and the absent bridges.

Navigating those unforgiving roads, we did have the good fortune of spotting a light green Land Rover Discovery2, with an ensign waving on its bonnet coming toward us. The King was in the passenger seat, he gave us a smile and a friendly wave as he passed by; he's obviously a Landy fan.

The King in his Disco

By-passing the craters and absent bridges we were surprised to eventually find we were on tarmac all the way to the town of Mongu where we set up camp. Mongu was like Land Rover City, there were so many of all shapes, sizes and ages lying around; Landy-Luck obviously led us to Mongu.

'Landy City'

It was time to replenish our food supplies so off to the local supermarket, Shoprite, we go but oops, they were on strike.

At long last we were almost within site of the Liuwa Plains. Liuwa being the Lozi word for Plain. We had to take two ferries on the way, one across the Zambezi, the other over the Luanginga river.

The first ferry was no problem, a well-managed and organised crossing. The next, over the Luanginga was another story. We eventually arrived at the boarding point, once we found it. Just two steel ramps lay on the sandy bank, no sign of a ferry boat. After much peering across the river we espied a small craft in the distance.

After waving, the boat set off toward us drawing up by the ramps. A price was agreed with the amiable skipper and my

The one out-board motored ferry

Landy, Fixer and I were welcomed aboard; there being space for just the one vehicle. Off we went chugging across the river, powered by one small outboard motor.

Making it to the other side we off loaded and parked my Landy a little way up the bank, making space for Les to bring his Landy ashore.

We were soon joined by some local kids offering to look after the Landy for us. They were a bundle of fun, and most grateful for the sweets we gave them.

The one out-board motored, ferry boat sailed back to collect Les and his Landy. Once loaded up they were on their way, but there

We'll look after your Landy

seemed some sort of delay. They were laid up amid-stream with Les, Caroline, Ollie and Amy aboard. What was going on? After a few minutes the ferry set off again, fortunately towards Fixer and me anxiously waiting for them.

Once on dry land, Les explained that the ferryman decided, as it was late of a Friday, he would up the fare by three times the price agreed. That **F**erry **D**elayed **PTI (FDPTI)** was soon sorted and the price stayed as first agreed. He was hoping to raise

Slightly dodgy ferryman

some extra cash to go out on the town with mates that evening.

Entering the Liuwa Plain National Park, we spent a considerable time at the gatehouse, filling in forms, paying fees and being well briefed about the Park. This is one of Africa's oldest conservation areas, first protected by the King of Barotseland back in 1880 then made a National Park in 1972. The Park is home to Wildebeest, Zebra, Gazelle, Wild Dog, Spotted Hyena, Cheetah, Elan, Tsessebe, and Roan Antelope. Lions, which were almost wiped out are now being re-introduced. The last Lioness, of the original family, Lady Liuwa, died of old age peacefully in 2012. Around three hundred and forty bird species also enjoy the freedom of the area.

We were given a map of the Park which we attempted to follow but it was 'gobble-de-gook' to us, so we simply trekked off northwards. Soon we were faced with yet another ferry crossing. This time it was all hands-on deck, as we helped the crew 'rope the boat ashore'.

Progress along the sandy trails over the plains was a real pleasure with wildlife popping in and out of our sight, taking absolutely no notice whatsoever. We came upon a young lady with a 15kg sack on her head, a baby on her back and a heavily packed carrier bag in one hand. We gave her a lift to her village, which happened to be on the way to our chosen campsite. As we set off Les arrived at one more **S**and **G**ottenstuk **PTI (SGPTI),** from which a quick tow soon had us on our way.

Some three quarters of an hour later we arrived at her village; what a struggle it would have been for her, but as she said, "I do it often". As she was getting out, she asked if we had any medicine to help her twelve-month-old baby, who wasn't very well with a temperature. Amongst our first aid items we found cough mixture and some antibiotics, which we handed to her with instructions on how to administer them to her youngster.

We, and the two Landys, were immediately surrounded by dozens of children and their parents. Young Ollie became star of the show, they all wanted to play with the little white boy. It really was a delightfully happy scene. I was re-christened, Doc. Martin!

Ollie with fans

Doc Martin

It was hard to leave those cheerful folks and move on.

Soon we arrived at another village which we drove through, got lost, went around in circles and ended up where we started back at the village. A young lad offered us help, he jumped into Les's Landy, guiding us out of the village and pointing us in the right direction. We then took the young navigator back to his village.

We did have Ethel, our Sat Nav on board, but she only showed us straight lines, with a disregard of the terrain or other obstacles in our path. Ethel had come with me from the UK, so I couldn't criticise her for being unfamiliar with the Plains where we were.

We settled down in the basic and remote Sikale Campsite, it was perfect for us to stopover and recuperate with the help of a braai and some vino. The birdsong during the evenings and early mornings, at this northern spot, was truly symphonic. How do they retain all those melodies in such a small brain?

Decamped and breakfasted, we set off to seek out some of the Liuwa's wildlife. We drove through hundreds of Wildebeest migrating slowly form north to south, a process they repeat the other way about, when the floods return; rather like the King.

A pair of ears popping up out of the grass attracted our attention. A Hyena was feasting upon the remains of a Wildebeest carcass. Soon, another hyena came along expecting to share the feast; he would have none of it seeing the uninvited guest off with a fierce attack.

One whole day we spent following Spotted Hyenas prowling through the plains. In

Hyena – mouth full

our now normal, don't quite know where we are way, we came across an abandoned Hyena Den. Several Hyena came running across the plains from different directions crossing in front of our Landys, they joined together and went off following each other, we followed; they didn't seem to mind. With now about a dozen in the group, we followed until they came to a halt on finding another Wildebeest carcass to be consumed. It must be their favourite, or perhaps most available dish.

Leaving them to enjoy their dinner, we followed a lone Hyena who took us to another inactive den, from its condition it was obvious they had only very recently moved out. The area we were in was so populated by Hyena that most other game kept well away, for fear of their lives.

We left the Park through the Kafue Gate. On the way to the gate we passed through one of the many small villages to find the area waterlogged. Not sure where the road was a local guy jumped up onto my rock slider and navigated us through mud and water. He was happy to be dropped off at the next village, and we carried on.

Soon we found ourselves not in floods, but in dry

Navigator

burning bush. From flood we had to drive through fire as fast as we were able. Both Landys made it with just a little damage, the seed screen on Les' Landy caught fire and melted away. We experienced the combined experiences of **F**lood, **M**ud and **F**ire **PTI (FMFPTI)** almost at the same time.

Through fire

Taking another ferry, we left the Park, driving east looking for somewhere to camp. The route now followed the main tarmac M9 road eastwards. Time was marching on, darkness fell, and we still hadn't found a campsite or accommodation of any sort. Driving this busy road in the dark it was another experience. My rule when in strange places, is not to drive after dark. This road was busy with large, heavily loaded, trucks trundling along in both directions. As the roadsides are taken up mainly by pedestrians, mopeds and cyclists with no lights the truckers keep very close to the central white line. Keeping their off-side indicators flashing enables them to pass each other at close quarters in the middle of the carriageway.

By around midnight we had suffered enough of this **N**ightmare **H**ighway **PTI (NHPTI)** so we pulled into a side road, found a wide kerb and bedded down. Caroline and Ollie kipped down in Les' roof top tent, the rest of us stretched out in our Landys.

Following our rather disturbed night, we set off toward our camping goal for the next night, the Kaingu Lodge. The Lodge is described as set in a wonderful location, just across the Kafue river on the threshold of the Kafue National Park, near Itezhi Tezhi.

We made good progress on that same busy main road during daylight. It felt like being back home in the UK having returned from a far-off alien planet. Before turning off the main road toward the campsite my Landy needed fuel. Fixer and I carried on to the town of Mumbwa to fill up while the others went to the Kaingu Lodge to prepare the campsite. Pulling up at a filling station in town the attendant said, "Sorry, we are out of diesel". "There are no other fuel stops around", he then went on to say, "I do have some diesel at my house if you want it". I am sure this was just another scam but left with little choice we took up his offer.

Was he in league with the scammers encountered earlier? He jumped into the Landy, directed us to his house, where with a mate, brought out several cans of the many we saw stacked in the bath. I checked the fuel, to be sure it was not diluted with water; it was after all stored in the bath! Finding it OK he filled the Landy at this **B**athroom **D**iesel **R**efuelling **PTI (BDRPTI)**.

Now it had to be paid for, no card reader in his bathroom, no cash in our pockets, the fuel was now in the Landy's tank. We

Bathroom filling station

took him back into town, withdrew cash from an ATM, paid him off and took him back to his bathroom. In my mind I am sure the fuel was stolen from the pumps at the filling station. How else, without the resources, or perhaps from scamming friends, do you fill your bath with diesel? I wondered what taking a bath in diesel must be like; it might clean the Landy grease off.

Back on the road we made it to The Kaingu Lodge, it was every bit as wonderful as described. Our friends were settled in, enjoying a coffee on the terrace overlooking the Kafue river, with Hippos for company. As I was asking Amy had she organized a spot for our tent, they all started giggling. "Yes, I have, it's that house over there", she laughingly replied and pointed. It was the most magnificent property on the estate, with a balcony overlooking the river and beyond into the wooded Kafue Park. An elephant was keeping his eye on us over the rocks from across the river. It was the most expensive property on the site.

Eventually I forgave Amy as it was so amazing; and found all the facilities at the Lodge to be excellent. Unfortunately, fixer was

Kaingu Lodge

left in the tent on his own for the night with grazing hippos for company; his night was as he put it was, somewhat 'disturbed'.

The words in their brochure I found to be spot on: -

The Kafue is one of the last true wilderness areas.
Covering 22,440km², its unmatched variety of species
and being able to enjoy the wildlife almost on your own,
makes this park one of the last secrets of Africa.
This is a place to unwind, enjoy our chefs' cuisine and
be spoiled with an abundance of activities
or, if you prefer, just relax and feel the heartbeat of Africa.

We enjoyed sundowners on the river watching the crocodiles, hippos and an angry elephant cavorting around. Back at the Lodge we enjoyed a sumptuous dinner, joined by the owners, with staff all around who joined with us in much chit chat. Following a very comfortable **L**uxurious **K**aingu **N**ights **PTI (LKNPTI)** night's sleep, apart from Fixer, we left Kaingu Lodge.

Amy, Fixer and I planned to go on the Vic Falls, while Les and Caroline, for timing and personal reasons, needed to make their way back to the Western Cape. Then, recalling another of our overlanding unwritten rules; 'travel together -never alone', unless necessary, so we revised our plans and made our way toward the Namibian Border together. We'll come back to the Falls another time.

Soon after leaving the Lodge we found ourselves in a heavily wooded area. It was such a change to be driving a track through delightful woodland. Deep in the woods we came upon a man with a broken-down bicycle; it was Nelson, one of the Lodge staff. He was on his way home from work riding his bike, when the ball bearings fell out of the pedal crank and he still had some 20km to go. Not able to fix the bike, onto the roof rack it went. We jumped back into the Landy, with Nelson sitting comfortably in the front passenger seat.

While we were stopped, with doors open, several unexpected and unwelcomed passengers joined our company; Tsetse Flies. Try as we might, it was impossible to swat the little devils; they are like bullets. Instant panic reigned. Amy found our can of Doom, so with all windows closed, she sprayed almost the whole contents of the can around the inside of the Landy.

This **T**setse **F**ly **PTI (TFPTI)** with Doom killed the tsetse flies and almost finished us off too; the spray was running down the windows.

A speedy recovery saw us on the way to Nelson's home which he was proud to show us; he built it himself for him, his wife and two kids. It was an attractive well-built home, a **N**elson **H**ome **PTI (NHPTI)**.

Nelson then asked us if we could take him to where his wife was working, a further fifteen km or so away; he was planning on getting there on his bike. Onwards we went, taking Nelson and his bike, stopping on the way, at one of the ubiquitous Mr. Patel's shops, to buy his cigarettes,

Nelson at home

Eventually we arrive at a 'T' junction with a tarred road where we turned right. Not far along, three bikes went pedalling past us in the opposite direction. "Stop, that's my wife and kids on their way home" he said. We off-loaded Nelson and his bike; once more we attempted to make a temporary repair for him, so he could catch up to his family. Not having any luck Nelson decided to push the bike to someone along the road to get his **N**elson **B**ike **PTI (NBPTI)** repaired and join the family later.

With Nelson's bike aboard

Unable to do more for Nelson we continued our way, staying at a campsite on the Nanzhila plains for the night. Amy, by way of penance for spending a fortune the night before, pitched our tent all on her own; a first!

Happily, it was Dirt road next day all the way to the border crossing at Katima Mulilo. At one point Les had to stop as a warning light was glowing on his dashboard. We think his Landy was suffering from being an **O**verheated **L**andy **PTI (OLPTI)**.

I towed him for about 10km after which it had it cooled down and there were no further heating issues.

Without any further setbacks we were soon back in the Okavango Delta. It was rather disappointing to be on the tarmac, as we sped toward our next night's destination, Ngepi Camp at Divundu on the banks of the Cumbango River. Ngepi was so good we stayed for an **E**xtra **N**gepi **N**ights **S**tay **PTI (ENNSPTI)**, despite Les and Caroline's need to be on the way. I'm sure it was me, our perhaps Ollie and Amy, that convinced them to rest up a while longer.

The accommodation was wonderful. My bathroom, The Kings Throne, was open air, set on the riverside with hippos playing in the river right in front of me. I enjoyed a bath, looking over my toes at those happy hippos, the 'Throne', whilst sitting on it, shared the same panorama. Ollie enjoyed a swim in the 'Hippo and Crocodile cage'. We all agreed the camp was well set out, fun, artistic, imaginative, entertaining and above all restful and unique. Early in the morning we were joined by Buffalo watching us from over the river.

Bath time at Ngepi

We reluctantly left Ngepi, with some 500km to cover before arriving once more at Berrybush Farm in Botswana. It was freezing cold when we arrived, so enjoyed a quick Braai by the fire and early to bed. Followed next day by an early start and drive across the border into Namibia, with no problems at all.

Making it to Windhoek, the girls 'went shopping', then found our campsite, Arebbusch, a recommended campsite.

Sadly, we had been directed to an 'annex' site. We spent a very **A**rebbusch **D**eafening **N**ights **PTI (ADNPTI)** right beside the side of the busy main B1 highway. The traffic noise did help getting us off to an early start in the morning. About 10km down the road we saw another Arebbusch Campsite, this looked very good, yes, we had indeed camped at the overflow annex.

Our sights were now set on the Fish River Canyon, breaking the journey with a night's rest in a lodge en-route. We met a guy hitching a lift, he was hoping to get to Ais-Ais. Not wishing to drop him off in the middle of nowhere, we mutually agreed it better for him to keep thumbing where he was.

Soon we found our intended rest spot for the night, a room right behind a filling station. Thank you, but no, we've had enough of deafening sleep-overs. So, on we went making it all the way to the Fish River Canyon. Stopping off to enjoy the sunset looking over Hells Corner in the canyon. A wonderful sight is this deep canyon, some five hundred-million-years old, not that it was this deep all those years back, and it's still working on making itself even deeper.

Setting up camp nearby we met the fellow we didn't give a lift to the day before. We started chatting around the braai to discover he, Dave, hailed from Sheffield, which happens to be Les and Caroline's home town; it is a very small world! Dave had been doing voluntary work in Malawi for a year or so and now decided he wanted to see more of Africa before going home. Dave, we found out was a keen Landyite, doing off-road days back in the UK in his Defender. He was hoping to get to Cape Town so, from that moment on, we added an extra member to our team. Landy-Luck certainly did him a good turn.

Leaving Fish River, we crossed back into South Africa, again without any problem, stopping off briefly at Springbok. A little further down the road, Fixer made a sudden stop and made a U-turn. There had been an incident, Police were at the scene. A bakkie and trailer had veered off the road and down a bank. A good Landy rescue opportunity.

Bakkie and trailer rescue

We winched the bakkie and trailer back onto the road by way of a **B**akkie and **T**railer **R**ecovery **PTI (BTRPTI)** by Landy.

All was well, they were on their way and we were able to continue our Landy way. Happily, no one was injured.

The last night of this adventure we spent in luxury at the Clanwilliam Lodge, where we were well fed, watered and rested. Rising later than normal next morning, we set off, visiting the Gateway Land Rover centre in Wellington on our way. Known as Nekkies. Gateway is a well-known repairer and restorer of Landys of all shapes, sizes and ages. Always good for a **G**ateway **N**ekkies **PTI (GNPTI)** stop, just to view the collection of Landys of various guises in the yard. I once bought a Zenith carburettor for Boudie from them which I was unable to find in the UK where Boudie was living at the time.

A while ago I, met Nekkie, from Gateway, at the famed Kelmarsh Land Rover Show in the UK. He had just driven a BMW V8 powered Defender all the way from home in Wellington to arrive in the main ring at the show. Wisely he had taken the more sensible route up the East Coast, not that it was **PTI** free. He and his 110 were the feature of a presentation in the main ring, along with Patrick Cruywagen, the editor of Land Rover Monthly. Patrick later wrote an interesting account of the trip in the Land Rover monthly magazine.

Our drive home from Wellington, was a straightforward cruise on the tarmac.

"Thank you" Land Rover for all the amazing
Land Rover 'Experiences'

Land Rover have many 'Experience Centres' around the world. I just create a few of my own from time to time.

Landy-Luck was with us all the time.

To her and all our Landy friends a very big thank you for all your help, friendship and support.

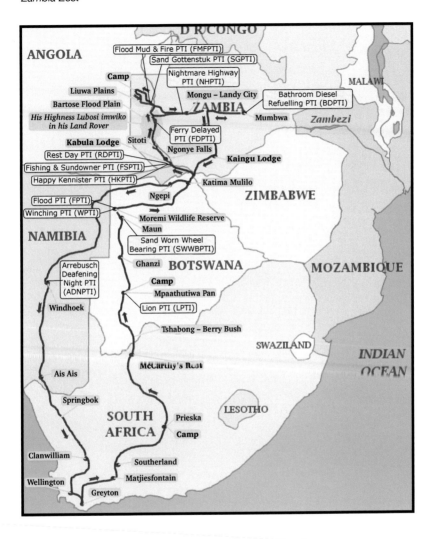

Chapter 36
A Few Landy 'Wisecracks'

Land Rovers are the targets of so many jokes, jibes, wisecracks and one-liners. Landy faith elevates we owners above them all!!
Some examples – some true – some fibs: -

Eighty percent of all Land Rovers ever built
are still on the road:
The other twenty percent made it home.

If there is no oil under a Land Rover
there is none in it.

Land Rovers don't leak oil.
They mark their territory.
(Or perhaps ooze energy)

Land Rover owners go straight to Heaven when they die.
They've had so much Hell on earth.

According to a recent poll ninety-eight percent
of people are dissatisfied with their lives.
The other two percent are Land Rover owners.

What is the difference between a Land Rover and a Porcupine?
Porcupines have pricks on the outside.

Land Rover have been turning owners into mechanics for 70yrs.

What do you call a Series Landy with brakes?
Customized.

My Land Rover didn't leak oil.
So the factory took it back and worked on it until it did.

Did I park my Land Rover, or is it broken down?

I'd rather push a Landy than drive Jap crap.

Unlike a Porsche, you can drive a Landy to its limits
and never get a ticket!

Standing on the roof of a Landy with a chainsaw
is the only way to trim trees.

So, you're in sixth form and you drive a Range Rover?
You must know all about hard work then.

What does the Titanic and a Land Rover have in common?
It has the same turning circle and is just as waterproof.

Why did they use Land Rovers for the Camel trophy?
To make things as difficult as possible for the contestants.

Why does a Land Rover have so many holes in it?
To let the water out.

When you mount a portrait of a Land Rover against the wall,
Remember to put newspapers on the floor to soak up the oil leaks.

You know it's a Land Rover when you stop at the fuel station and
ask the attendant to check the fuel level and fill up the oil.

All Land Rovers are like women.
They leak when you don't want them to, moan on long journey's,
embarrass you in front of friends and spend more money than you
ever expected once you've committed yourself to one.

There are two man-made structures visible from space:
The Great Wall of China and
The gap in a defender's door frame.'

A Toyota owning friend once told me he would buy a Landy.
If he was able to open the window 'after' he got in.

You can always get spares
No matter where you are in the world.

Landys can park on the kerb (when others can't!)

Landys can make a U-turn and drive over the kerb!!!

There is nothing more instantly recognisable than a Landy!

Why spend a fortune on the newest sport utility today?
You can spend much more on a Series IIA over 20 years.

You have seen the rest now...now drive the best...

I could keep going for ever; but I won't.

Chapter 37
PTI – The Truth

In Land Rovers defence, I have prepared an analysis, gathered from the previous chapters, of the various reasons for

Progress being Temporarily Impeded **(PTI)**

My tales contain some 122 incidents of **PTI**, only 13 (10.7%) could be attributed to any form of mechanical failure. Some, such as Silencer and exhausts falling, off should really be attributed to owner lack of maintenance.

I have broken down my experience **PTI** into the following categories and percentages of Impediment overall –

CATEGORY	PTI No:	PTI%	PTI Description:
Mechanical:	13	10%	Repairs/adjustment etc.
Operator Error:	16	13%	Driver errors
Officialdom:	21	17%	Security, Customs etc.
Unexpected:	24	20%	Other incidents.
Recovery	10	8%	Recovering Toyotas.
Pure Fun:	38	31%	Pure fun stops.
	122		

My results show most reasons for **P**rogress being **T**emporarily **I**mpeded. Far more genuine reasons than the subjects of all the jokes, jibes, gags wisecracks and one-liners you may hear.

The following tables categorise the various **PTI**:-

'Mechanical'- PTI

1	No Steering PTI (NSPTI)	Disco1 V8 Steering column broke.	Botswana
2	Steering Pump PTI (SPPTI)	Faulty Power Steering pump. Disco1 V8.	
3	Kalahari Clutch PTI (KCPTI)	Defender Td5 clutch slipping.	Kalahari
4	Burst Pipe PTI (BPPTI)	Disco 300tdi heater pipe.	France
5	French Disconnection PTI (FDPTI)	Series III Lwt: broke synchromesh.	
6	Shock Absorber PTI (SAPTI)	Disco1 Td3.	
7	Shock Absorbing PTI (SAPTI)	Series III Lwt: Shocker bracket broke.	Tunisia
8	Jockey Wheel Bearing PTI (JWBPTI)	Defender Td3. Fan belt tensioner jockey wheel bearing worn.	Mozambique
9	Smokey Turbo PTI (STPTI)	Td3 Hybrid. Turbo bearings failed.	Wales
10	Sand Worn Wheel Bearing PTI (SWWBPTI)	Defender 110 Td3: Wheel bearing.	Botswana
11	Overheated Landy PTI (OLPTI)	Defender Td5: Overheated.	Zambia
12	Make-Over PTI (MOPTI)	Series III Lwt: Given a 'face-lift'.	South Africa
13	Desert Stormer PTI (DSPTI)	Boudie having suspension softened.	

'Operator Error' – PTI

1	Out Of Fuel PTI (OFPTI)	Lack of vigilance.	Botswana
2	Shafting PTI (SPTI)	Over scoring half shafts – off-roading.	UK
3	Silencer PTI (SPTI)	Disco Td3 Lost silencer. Poor maintenance.	Botswana
4	Muffler PTI (MPTI)	Disco Td3 Lost silencer. Poor maintenance.	
5	Show-Off-Operator (SOOPTI)	No more to be said! It was me showing off, stuck in a donga.	Greyton, SA
6	Botswana Puncture PTI (BPPTI)	Taking short cut.	Botswana
7	Gottenstuk and Winching PTI (GWPTI)	Disco1. Stuck in sand.	Tunisia
8	Puncture PTI (PPTI)	Puncture Algeria.	Algeria
9	Sand Gottenstuk PTI (SGPTI)	Stuck in sand.	
10	Nightmare Highway PTI (NHPTI)	2 x Defenders Failed to find campsite.	Zambia
11	Bathroom Diesel Refuelling PTI (BDRPTI)	Low fuel reserves – Lack of attention.	
12	Arebbusch Deafening Nights PTI (ADNPTI)	Picking wrong 'noisy' Campsite by main road.	Botswana
13	Widow Maker PTI (WMPTI)	Fixer's sad accident when missing a gear.	Wales
14	Cold Wet River TPI (CWRTPI)	I Tipped Hybrid over in cold river.	
15	Desert Stormer PTI (DSPTI)	Getting stuck during 'Heritage' weekend.	South Africa
16	Silencer PTI (SPTI)	Disco Td3 Lost silencer.	Botswana

'Officialdom' – PTI

1	**Delayed Boarding (DBPTI)**	Delay at Dover.	UK
2	**Polizia Door PTI (PDPTI)**	Door into office at Genoa – no handle!	Italy
3	**Border Control Meddling and Confiscation (BC&MCPTI)**	Lwt & Disco1. Thorough search. Confiscation of radios and other items.	Algeria
4	**SH*1*T PTI (SH1TPTI)**	Encircled by army troops on exercise.	
5	**'Irritability' PTI (IPTI)**	Constant Security checks.	
6	**Al-Qaeda PTI (AQPTI)**	Al-Qaeda activates preventing access into Niger.	
7	**Niger Border PTI (NBPT)**	Border closure.	
8	**'Hasslement' PTI (HPTI)**	Security and driving restrictions.	
9	**Irritation and Frustration PTI (I&FPTI)**	Escort out of the country with military escort.	
10	**PTI by Swiss Agent (SAPTI)**	The remote agent not aware of the situation in the country.	
11	**Fake Police PTI (FPPTI)**	A compulsory Police Escort was not so.	
12	**U-TURN PTI (UTPTI)**	Turnaround of attitude by customs.	
13	**Returned Confiscated Goods PTI. (RCGPTI)**	Time spent waiting for the return of goods taken.	
14	**Libyan Entry Visa PTI (LEVPTI)**	Libyan visa granted, entry not permitted till Egyptian visa agreed.	Libya
15	**Procrastinating PTI (PPTI)**	Time spent obtaining visas and changing route.	
16	**Ethiopian No Entry PTI (ENEPTI)**	Visa refused as entry to Ethiopia refused due to civil war.	Egypt
17	**Waiting In Tripoli PTI (WITPTI)**	Time Lwt spent in Tripoli waiting to be shipped.	Algeria

18	Boudie Rotterdam PTI (BRPTI)	Lwt waiting in Rotterdam, when told not possible to ship to Europe.	Netherlands
19	Long Wait Shipping PTI (LWSPTI)	Waiting for Lwt; to arrive in Cape Town.	South Africa
20	Access Permit PTI (APPTI)	Entry into Namaqualand.	
21	Food Loss PTI (FLPTI)	Meat taken from us Vet. Barrier.	Botswana

'Unexpected Circumstance' – PTI

1	Bank Holiday PTI (BHPTI)	Arrive LR Garage Maun Local Bank Holiday!	Botswana
2	Plane Delay (PDPTI)	Parts failed to arrive – Pilot overslept.	
3	Halal PTI (HLPTI)	Ritual cattle kill in road.	Namibia
4	Chain Saw Massage (CSPTI) (Not quite a 'Massacre')	Unexpected accident to member of proposed team.	UK
5	Gall-Bladder PTI (GB-PTI)	Unexpected illness.	
6	Laundered PTI (LPTI)?	Rained on laundry.	Italy
7	Pot Hole PTI (PHPTI)	Huge potholes.	Moz.
8	Map Reading PTI (MRPTI)	Basic GPS useless in Desert.	Sahara
9	Key Board (KBPTI)	Arabic and French only keyboards in Internet Café.	Algeria
10	Libyan Fuel PTI (LFPTI)	Unofficial fuel supplies	Libyan border
11	Better Value Libyan Cash PTI (BVLCPTI)	Great Money Exchange.	
12	Traffic PTIs (MTPTI)	Traffic chaos.	Moz.
13	Coca Cola PTI (CCPTI)	Store out of supplies.	Wuppertal
14	Cheetah Dinner PTI (CDPTI)	Baboon carcass on doorstep.	Die Hell
15	A Stinking Dead Cow PTI (SDDCPTI)	Putrid cow carcass at roadside.	Karoo

16	Lion **PTI (LPTI)**	Lion sits outside tent roaring.	Kgalagadi
17	Lion **T**in **O**pener **PTI (LTOPTI)**	After being told how easily a lion could open a tent.	
18	Ferry **D**elayed **PTI (FDPTI)**	Mid river fee negotiations for ferry crossing.	Zambia
19	**I**nsulating **PTI (IPTI)**	Adding heat insulation to Boudie.	France
20	**B**roken **C**oncrete **T**rack **(BCTPTI)**	Wuppertall broken concrete track.	South Africa
21	Tsetse **F**ly **PTI (TFPTI)**	Tsetse flys in Lany.	Zambia
22	**N**elson **B**ike **PTI (NBPTI)**	Help Nelson with Bicycle.	
23	**P**uncture **PTI (PPTI)**	Puncture.	Algeria
24	**P**uncture **PTI (PPTI)**	Puncture.	Botswana

'Recovery' – PTI

1	**S**alt **P**an **PTI (SPPTI)**	Boudie recovers Tasca from Saltpan.	Tunisia
2	Heritage **R**ecovery **PTI (HRPTI)**	Boudie recovered from Donga, SA 4x4 Heritage Day.	Greyton
3	**L**impopo **PTI (LPTI)**	Toyota and LR110 winched from Limpopo River.	Moz.
4	**C**oconut **TPI (CPTI)**	Toyota Bakkie loaded with coconuts winched from mud.	
5	Third **P**arty **O**ut **O**f **F**uel **PTI (TPOOFPTI)**	Gave fuel to bus on dirt road.	Lesotho
6	**D**oor **L**ocked **PTI (DLPTI)**	Rescued myself, having locked keys in 110.	South Africa
7	**B**akkie and **T**railer **R**ecovered **PTI (BTRPTI)**	Winched Bakkie and trailer from bank off main road.	
8	**M**onaco **GP PTI (MGPPTI)**	Driving Boudie and Tasca around part of F1 circuit.	Monaco
9	**S**alty **PTI (SPTI)**	Rock Roses in Salt Pans.	Tunisia
10	**T**oyota **L**andy **R**escue **PTI (TLRPTI)**	Rescuing Toyota from escarpment.	Wales

'Fun' - PTI

1	**W**ine **C**ocktail **PTI** (**WCPTI**)	Helper at campsite accepts and rapidly drinks some 5L mixture of split red and white wines and water recovered from fridge.	Namibia
2	**R**eno **PTI? (RPTI)**	Should we recover two war damaged LRs left to rot.	
3	**B**ubbly **PTIs (BPTI)**	Unexpected party time at Champagne Festival.	France
4	**S**ynchro **& C**hampagne **PTI (S&C PTI)**	Treated to champagne by LR garage in Rodez after fixing Boudie's synchro.	
5	**F**un **PTI (FPTI)**	Pure fun scaling sand dunes.	Tunisia
6	**L**eisure **PTI (LPTI)**	Sand, sights & Potholes.	
7	**B**rew **PTI (BPTI)**	Brewing tea gets us stuck in soft sand – Great Fun.	Algeria
8	**B**aking **PTIs (BPTI)**	Fun with the local Tuareg people. Baking in the sand, eating with them. How to make tea the desert way.	
9	**E**ating **PTI (EPTI)**		
10	**T**ea **TPI (TTPI)**		
11	**C**itroen **(CPTI)**	Visiting Citroen House and Palmier.	
12	**P**leasant **O**asis **PTI (POPTI)**	Enjoying amazing oasis in desert.	Sahara
13	**H**ermitage **PTI (HPTI)**	Visit Hermitage in Hoggard Mts.	Algeria
14	**G**ite **S**aharien **(GSPTI)**	Pleasant stopover at Niger border.	
15	**C**amel **R**oad **T**est **PTI (CRTPTI)**	Road Test Camel vs Landy.	
16	**R**esting **PTI (RPTI)**	Stay at Hamed's Auberge and music festival .	
17	**H**ouse **H**unting **PTI (HHPTI)**	Spotting various house for reno.	Tunisa, Libya, Algeria
18	**A**rchery **C**ontest **PTI (ACPTI)**	Winning Archery competition.	Tunisia
19	**R**oman **L**eptis **M**agna **PTI (RLMPTI)** **R**oman **S**abratha **PTI (RSPTI)**	Visiting Roman ruins.	Libya

20	Land Rover and Classic Car PTI Calitzdorp Land Rover Festival	Time spent at Land Rover shows.	South Africa
21	Landy Badge PTI (LBPTI)	Obtaining Landy Badges from scrapped Series Landys.	Moz.
22	Real Estate PTI (REPTI)	Viewing derelict properties Cederberg.	South Africa
23	Amarula Kernel PTI (AKPTI)	Eating Amarula nut kernel taken from an elephant turd.	Umflozi
24	Tafelberg Veteran Trekker & Enjin Klub PTI (TVTEK)	With Boudie with new owner at a New Club Show.	Dortopia
25	Ecstatic PTIs (EPTI)	Visiting Hell.	Die Hell
26	Heaven In Hell PTI (HIHPTI)	In Hell again.	Die Hell
27	Vertigo PTI (VPTI)	On way into Baviaans Kloof.	South Africa
28	One-Legged PTI (OLPTI)	Watching Flamingos.	Tankwa Karoo
29	Martin Island PTI (MIPTI)	Staking my claim to island in the dam.	Tankwa Karoo
30	Flood PTI (FPTI)	Fun in mud and flood.	Moremi
31	Little Charitable PTI (LCPTI)	Fixer donating granddaughters old clothes to families.	Zambia
32	Landy Rest Day PTI (LRDPTI)	Extended stay at Kabula Lodge on Zambezi.	Zambia
33	Fishing and Sundowner PTI (FSPTI)	More fun at Kabula Lodge.	Zambia
34	Happy Kennister PTI (HKPTI)	Friendly local showing us around villages.	Zambia
35	Flood, Mud and Fire PTI (FMFPTI)	Driving through floods, mud and a fire on Liuwe Plains.	Zambia
36	Luxurious Kaingu Nights PTI (LKNPTI)	Amy's special stay in luxury at Kaingu Lodge.	Zambia
37	Extra Ngepi Nights Stay PTI (ENNSPTI)	Had to spend extra night at fabulous Ngepi Camp.	Namibia
38	Nelson Home PTI (NHPTI)	Visit to Nelson's home.	Zambia

If faith in an old Landy is good enough for Jim Ratcliffe – the UK's richest man and proud owner of a very early Series1 – then surely that is one good reason we should all have faith in Landys and live a **'Contented Landy Life'**.

Jim, we are all waiting for you to come up with a hardy, gizmo free 4x4 replacement for the older Land Rovers. The market is there all around the world where folk have the desire to live the good life.

> 'Faith in Land Rovers is the way to live that happy,
> contented and fulfilled Landy life'

Landy-Luck will always be there for you.

Don't rely on 'Hope' – Hope doesn't always happen.

I cannot thank Land Rover enough for taking me along this path.

'Enjoy a Happy Land Rovering Life'

ACKNOWLEDGEMENTS

How can I ever begin to say, "thank you" to the so many wonderful folks who helped me go 'Further by Far' and 'Above and Beyond'.

A big thank you to dear wife Christine, though not a devotee of my overlanding ways, she understands and puts up with my many dirty Landy liaisons.

The Camel Trophy contenders who spent many cold, wet and windy winter nights under canvass at Eastnor Castle estate, along with their instructors, who planted so many Landy way seeds.

My tales would not be, without my regular 'crews' made up of Richard (The Animal) and Monique Hess, not forgetting Richard Box (Fixer) a frequent off-roading buddy. I am very indebted to special good friend Paps who flew over from SA to join me and Boudie on the eventful, though later aborted, UK to SA overland trip. To John and Roz Onions, thanks for all your pre-trip help, sadly health hiccups grounded you; you remain my good friends.

A big thank you also to friends Les, Caroline and Ollie Glover who along with my Granddaughter Amy, made the Zambian experience so amazing. Thank you, Caroline for some wonderful photos.

Boudie would not have been mine but for Howard, who swapped her for a garden shed, so further fertilizing my maturing Landy ways.

Thank you, Bryn Hemming, for the time and effort spent working on my hybrids and making Chloe, Boudie and Tasca fighting fit. Also, John of 'Hot Wheels' in Greyton for Boudie's face-lift.

Very high on my list of friends and helpers are Schalk and Marlize Burger of Somerset West. They keep and have kept my

SA Landy wheels turning for many years. I cannot begin to list the efforts they continue with on my behalf.

The Land Rover garages at Maun, Gaborone and George also win praise for their stalwart efforts. Thank you, Juan Strauss of Windhoek, for your sterling efforts in supplying brake parts on the Skeleton Coast, also to the garage in Henties Bay who carried out the repairs.

I thank Louis Smit of Worcester 4x4 for softening Boudie's ride, also for his endless Landy wit. Just a shame he is a Toyota man.

Wikipedia have been very helpful in refreshing my memory and confirming some unsure facts; thanks.

A very special 'Thank you' to Claudia and Younus in Tamanrasset for their sterling efforts in helping us during those fraught times waiting and attempting to cross the border into Niger. Your help radiated throughout Algeria and beyond into Libya. You, and your wonderful Auberge will never be forgotten.

Also, to the many others, you are not forgotten.

I Thank You all.

A very special 'thank you' to my good friend Stuart Shearer,
who recently left this world to travel the next long journey
to the 'other side'.
It is a long trip; we will all be travelling the same road.
Don't let the clutch slip.
Maybe not in a Land Rover but I will catch up with you along
the same road in time.